*Creating An Impression* was written by **Basil Aldyman** with follicle stimulation from **Niall Clark** and **Colin Gilbert** and a pile of clippings from **Iain Campbell**, **Rab Christie & Greg Hemphill**, **Philip Differ**, **Alan Hay**, **Brendan McGeever & John McGlade**.

*The Baldy Man* is played by Gregor Fisher

First published in the UK in 1995 by
Boxtree Limited
Broadwall House
21 Broadwall
London SE1 9PL

10 9 8 7 6 5 4 3 2 1

Book designed by Nigel Davies, Stone Studio, London

Cover designed by Martin Lovelock

Cover photographs by Ken Mellin

Photography by Ken Mellin, Trevor Leighton, Alywn R. Coats, and Annie Peel

Printed and bound in Great Britain by Cambus Litho Ltd

ISBN: 0 7522 0678 8

A catalogue record for this book is available from the British Library

The Publishers would like to thank Polygram Video International, Polygram Television International, Ray Holman, Julie Dorrat-Keenan and Judith Barkas

# CREATING AN IMPRESSION

### BY

## BASIL ALDYMAN

WORKING TITLE
TELEVISION

B⊞XTREE

The **BALDY MAN**'s new video "Introducing" will be available early October from all good video stockists, price **£12.99** rrp.

What a suave fellow! & Ladies Beware!

Introducing...
**THE BALDY MAN**
PG

NEW LOOK DELEGATE
KEEP FIT ILL

PolyGram Video

'Prêt-A-Porter' look out!

Alternatively, order direct from:

**Video Plus Direct**
**P.O. Box 190**
**Peterborough**
**PE2 6UW**

**BY POST** enclosing a cheque made payable to **'VIDEO PLUS DIRECT'** for **£12.99 + £1.75** (Post and packaging)

or **BY CREDIT CARD** on **01733 232800**

# CREATING AN IMPRESSION

You've either got or you <u>haven't</u> got style, as the song goes. Fortunately, I've got it in spades. With my natural dress sense, poise and sparkling repartee I've got everything just right - in fact I've often heard people say "We've got a 'right' one here."

Now for the first time, in the pages of this book, I'm prepared to share the secrets of my success with you.

Section by section I answer the vital questions of etiquette and social skills which will give you the confidence to tackle life head on. Questions like: "What make of open toed sandals to wear with a dress suit!" "Which knife and fork to use at a finger buffet!" and "What jokes to tell on being introduced to the Queen at a garden party!" The answers to all these questions, and more, can be found within this treasury of taste!

After applying the knowledge learned in these meticulously researched pages you'll be amazed at how popular you have become! Invitations to take part in countless social activities will soon be dropping through your letterbox! The Readers Digest Prize Draw! Private Previews of Timeshare Properties! Recently I answered a fast food questionnaire where the first prize was a slap-up meal for two at Harry Ramsden's. (Though for some reason I was offered a slap-head meal for one at Hare Krishnas.)

'Creating an Impression' is a classic in the making. It will change your life. As a work on etiquette, social graces and breeding it ranks alongside such masterpieces as 'Burke's Peerage', 'Prat's Empire' and 'Complete Dunderhead's Aristocracy'. Read it today and become an ultimate style guru like me!

*Basil Aldyman*

Basil Aldyman.

P.S. If within ten days of following the advice in this book you do not find people staring in admiration as you pass, stepping aside to make way for you in shops and smiling as they discuss you with their friends, then you have my personal assurance and guarantee... that you're a complete no-hoper and just don't have 'it'.

# Tracing One's Ancestry

**You only have to look at my picture to realise that Breeding Counts! In any social situation I seem to have a little something that sets me apart from the crowd.**

However, although it's obvious from my appearance that I come from a noble, aristocratic lineage, I am constantly amazed at the number of people who refuse to accept this on the evidence of their eyes alone!! The simple truth is if you want to create an impression in today's social whirl, tracing your ancestry is the only answer.

## How To Go About It

Start with your closest ancestral relative and check for any family resemblances. In my case although they **are** there, they're very hard to spot.

Next examine family documents such as birth certificates. These are constant, treasured reminders of the happy arrival of a new addition to the family. Strangely enough, I discovered mine had been destroyed by my mother.

This forced me to visit the public records office at St Catherine's House. At first they tried to fob me off by saying my family had no connection with the nobility. Fortunately – and all thanks to my own efforts – I was able to uncover a simple genealogical table which clearly links me with the crowned heads of Europe. (See facing page.)

## The Trappings Of Lineage!

If like me you are an officially recognised member of the aristocracy you're entitled to have your own Coat of Arms. This should be in the traditional colours of red, blue and gold with a design of hunting hounds, trumpets and griffins heads – not an easy material to come by. Fortunately I have a pair of pyjamas in exactly this pattern.

Finally, as the icing on the cake, you should choose a Family Crest with a Motto – something which sums up one's entire attitude to oneself. I simply got a local artist to paint an appropriate design. I love it!

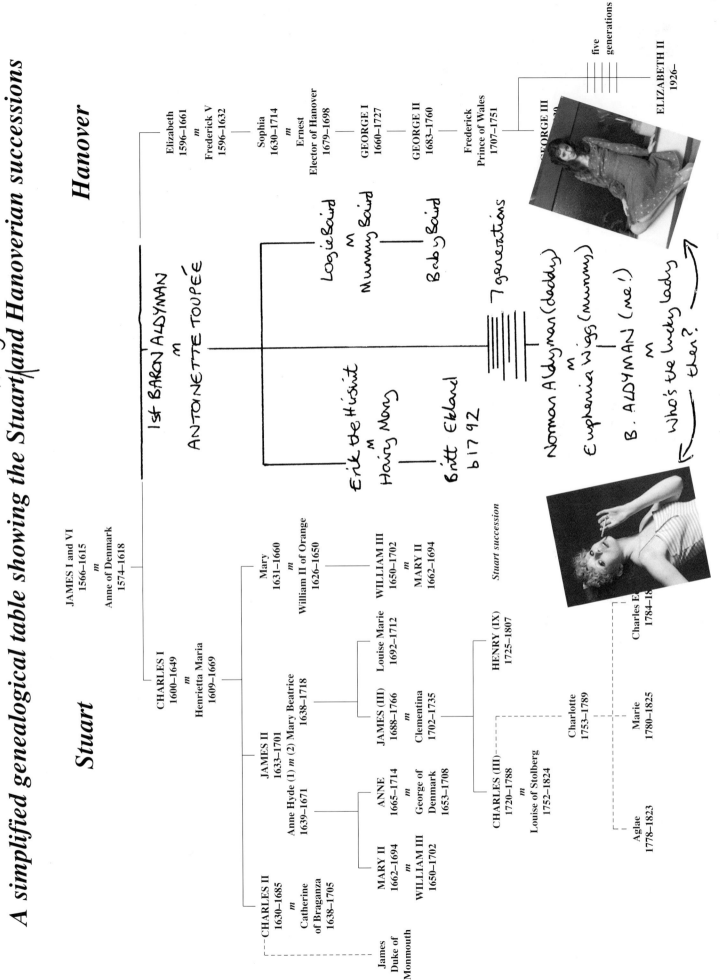

Aldyman

# A simplified genealogical table showing the Stuart and Hanoverian successions

# Acquire Superior Skills

**SPEAK A FOREIGN LANGUAGE**

How often have you wished you could be fluent in a foreign language!? French, perhaps, for, as we know, French is the language of lurrve!! What better way to set female hearts a-flutter than by whispering a few 'sweet nothings' or – as a master of foreign languages like myself might say – 'bonbon riens' into her ear. But then, to use another French expression, I'm just a Gigolo!

*Just a Gigolo!* →

## NO PROFESSIONAL TUITION NECESSARY

Learning your chosen foreign language the A.S.S. way requires no professional tuition – just my expert advice!

First, ignore all those other 'Teach Yourself' courses which tell you to learn a foreign language the way you learned English. What nonsense! I don't want to spend another ten years sitting at a schooldesk listening to Batty Battersby droning on about Shakespeare whilst Stinko Wilkins fires ink pellets down my neck!

## LISTEN AND LEARN

With the A.S.S. languages course you simply learn by listening to records. Each course consists of three professionally prepared foreign language records, selected by myself, designed to help YOU become more fluent in the language of your choice!

**ITALIAN!**
SHADDAP YA FACE!
LIFE IS A MINESTRONE
JUST ONE CORNETTO

**FRENCH!**
QUE SERA, SERA
CHANSON D'AMOUR
MADEMOISELLE FROM ARMENTIERES

**SPANISH!**
Y VIVA ESPANA
HERNANDO'S HIDEAWAY
AGADOO

**OUTER MONGOLIAN**
OO WAKKA DOO WAKKA DAY
SUPERCALIFRAGILIS TICEXPIALIDOCIOUS
REMEMBER YOU'RE A WOMBLE

If you don't have a record player then tick the box marked 'TAPES PLEASE!' and I'll send you specifically prepared tape recordings of these records made using the most advanced sound equipment.

TAPES, PLEASE

# WHERE TO USE YOUR SKILLS

## THE RESTAURANT!

Go to your favourite French or Italian restaurant and see how surprised and delighted the waiters are when you you are able to order the food IN THEIR OWN LANGUAGE! You might order 'Pizza' in Italian for instance or 'Hors D'Ouvres' in French!

When you're ordering your meal using your new foreign language skills always speak loudly enough for other diners to hear. Most of them won't be able to read the menu themselves and will be impressed by your knowledge and secretly grateful for your help!

## THE FOREIGN FILMHOUSE!

Having mastered a foreign language you will be able to get much more enjoyment out of foreign films at the cinema – mainly because you will be able to point out to other filmgoers where the subtitles are wrong!

I myself have tried this and after showing the man sitting next to me only three eroneous subtitles he got up and walked out in disgust! I'm not surprised. Such sloppy film-making shouldn't be allowed.

## IN THE STREET!

But you don't have to be in a restaurant or at the pictures to try out your new language. Now that you're a fluent speaker you can use it anywhere. Simply find two native speakers of the language you've learned having a conversation in the street. Creep up behind them and listen for a while. Then simply join in! Imagine their surprise and delight when they discover you can speak to them IN THEIR OWN LANGUAGE! You can often learn some new words that way too!

LISTEN

UNDERSTAND

JOIN IN!

SEE THEIR SURPRISE AND DELIGHT!

# SPOT THE BALL(DY)

All the people in the above crowd have a full head of hair except for one **BALD HEADED MAN** who has been cleverly removed from the picture. Using your skill and judgement place a cross where you think the centre of the **BALD HEADED MAN**'s cranium was.

The decision of the judges is final and no correspondence about other possible bald headed men will be entered into!

## LAST WEEK'S WINNER!
MR. B.ALDYMAN, "DUNCOMBIN", AXMINSTER AVENUE, RUGWICH

## LAST WEEK'S SOLUTION

# BODY LANGUAGE
## No.1 - THE OPPOSITE SEX

**People of the opposite sex often use non-verbal signals to convey their attraction to each other. My specially prepared 'Body Language' guide will help you make the right moves to gain the attention of that mysterious and special lady, ensnaring her in your debonair, devil-may-care spell before you've even said a word!**

♥ **1** The opening stance! Legs apart, thumbs tucked into tops of pockets! This says 'I am virile, I am macho, …I am probably single.'

♥ **2** Fondling an object suggestively can be a way of attracting a female's attention and letting her know 'you've got it!'

**3** Eye contact. Subtle use of eye contact will let her know your attention is focused on her!

**4** A cigarette can be a sensual giver of signals, but always blow your smoke up as this conveys confidence and superiority.

Smoke up - Confident, Superior.

Smoke down - Your trousers may be on fire.

**5** The way you angle your body sends a clear message to the object of your interest. Position yourself so you are almost imperceptively 'pointing' in her direction.

**6** Don't fold your arms as this can be interpreted as a negative gesture.

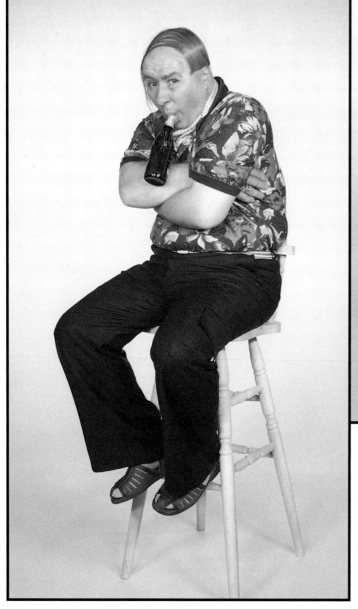

It also makes it very difficult to drink your beer.

**7** Facial gestures are crucial. Stroking the chin suggests an understanding nature.

**8** Hands behind the head indicates you are dominant and ready to make a move!

**9** Cross your legs with a foot pointing at the lady you want to impress.

 **10** Finally, let's put it all together!

**MR IRRESISTIBLE!**

# BADGES OF SOPHISTICATION

In certain social situations wearing an official badge can open doors for you. The process of applying for and being issued with one of these badges can be time consuming and frustrating, however. You'd be amazed at the number of times I've had my applications turned down – or even ignored – despite my excellent credentials! A simple, but effective, way round the problem is simply to make your own badge. All you need is a piece of stiff card and some Letraset. To give the general idea here are just some of the badges I've made up and worn as the occasion demanded.

**PRESS**

**CHIEF STEWARD**

**TEAM SKODA**

**V.I.P.**

**ROYAL EQUERRY E.R.**

**OFFICIAL PHOTOGRAPHER**

**VERY, VERY V.I.P.**

**U.N. DELEGATE**

**EXTRA ON BAYWATCH**

**MISS CARTLAND'S PARTY**

**N.A.S.A. FLYER**

**KISS ME QUICK**

**FRIEND OF VIDAL SASSOON**

**DOUBLE FOR STALLONE**

**BACKSTAGE PASS BEVERLY SISTERS TOUR**

**MILK MONITOR**

**A WORD OF WARNING** – Here are a few badges it's best NOT to wear.

**KICK ME**

**No. 7211584 WORMWOOD SCRUBS**

**FRIEND OF JEFFREY ARCHER**

# IMPRESSING THE NEIGHBOURS

Imagine you've just moved into a new house. How do you make that all-important lasting first impression on your new neighbour – especially if she turns out to be attractive, single and female!?

In my case, of course, I'm probably just the 'dreamboat' she's been longing for. So here's my tip for a simple way of starting up a perfect relationship!

EXCUSE ME, I'VE JUST MOVED IN NEXT DOOR AND I SEEM TO HAVE RUN OUT OF SHAMPOO

# MAKING THE MOST OF YOUR MAIL

Remember, your postman reads your mail as well as you – and will often tell the rest of the neighborhood about it.
Bear this in mind when you subscribe to Home Delivery magazines.

## MAGAZINES YOU SHOULD HAVE HOME DELIVERED

The Lancet
Wine Connoisseurs Weekly
The Stage
English Heritage
Le Monde
For Him
Loaded!
Classical Music Lover
What Patio
Cordon Bleu Cookery
Horse & Hounds

## MAGAZINES YOU SHOULD NOT HAVE HOME DELIVERED

Pigeon Fanciers Monthly
Cooking For One
Dating Agency Partners Update
Which Whippet
Bunty
Outsize Misfits Home Shopping Catalogue
Diet Monthly
Grimsby Town F.C. Fanzine
Pen Pals Weekly
Specially For Bald Gits

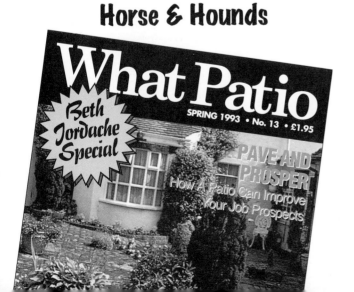

What Patio
Beth Jordache Special
SPRING 1993 • No. 13 • £1.95
PAVE AND PROSPER
How A Patio Can Improve Your Job Prospects

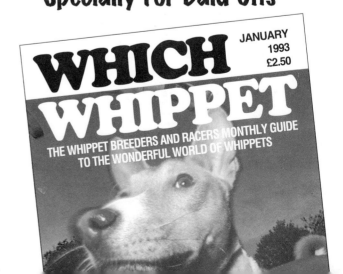

WHICH WHIPPET
JANUARY 1993 £2.50
THE WHIPPET BREEDERS AND RACERS MONTHLY GUIDE TO THE WONDERFUL WORLD OF WHIPPETS

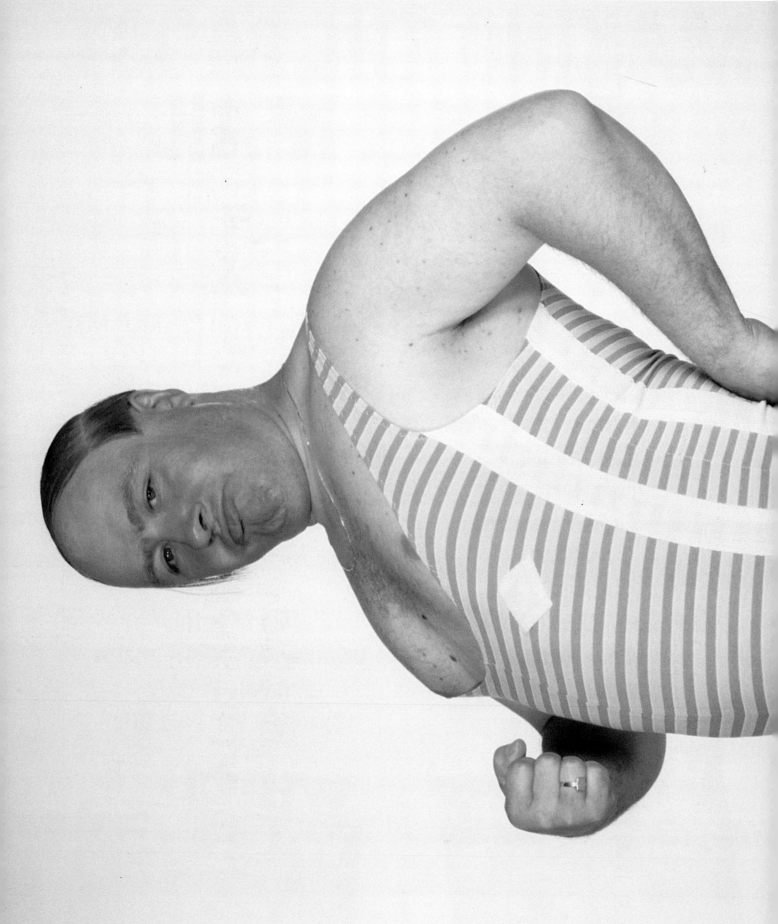

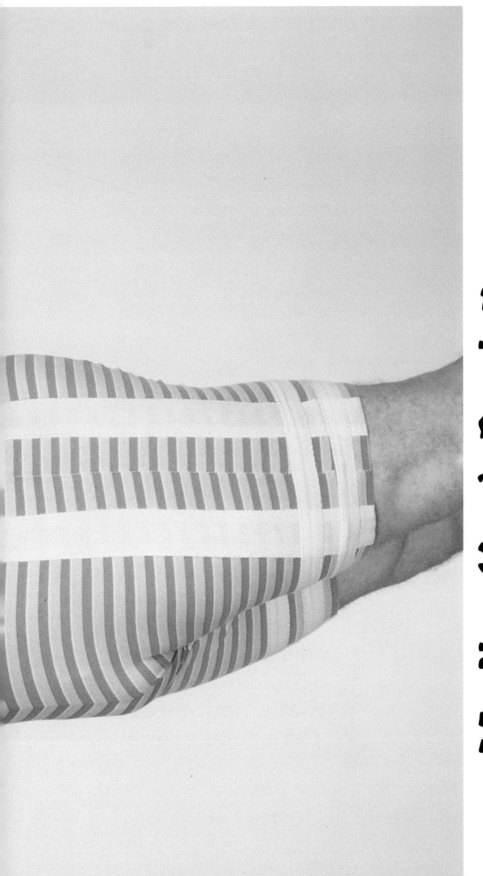

# My New Year's Resolution –
## to get in shape and join the Gladiators

| JANUARY | | | | | | |
|---|---|---|---|---|---|---|
| M | T | W | T | F | S | S |
| 1 | 2 | 3 | 4 | 5 | 6 | 7 |
| 8 | 9 | 10 | 11 | 12 | 13 | 14 |
| 15 | 16 | 17 | 18 | 19 | 20 | 21 |
| 22 | 23 | 24 | 25 | 26 | 27 | 28 |
| 29 | 30 | 31 | | | | |

| FEBRUARY | | | | | | |
|---|---|---|---|---|---|---|
| M | T | W | T | F | S | S |
| | | | 1 | 2 | 3 | 4 |
| 5 | 6 | 7 | 8 | 9 | 10 | 11 |
| 12 | 13 | 14 | 15 | 16 | 17 | 18 |
| 19 | 20 | 21 | 22 | 23 | 24 | 25 |
| 26 | 27 | 28 | 29 | | | |

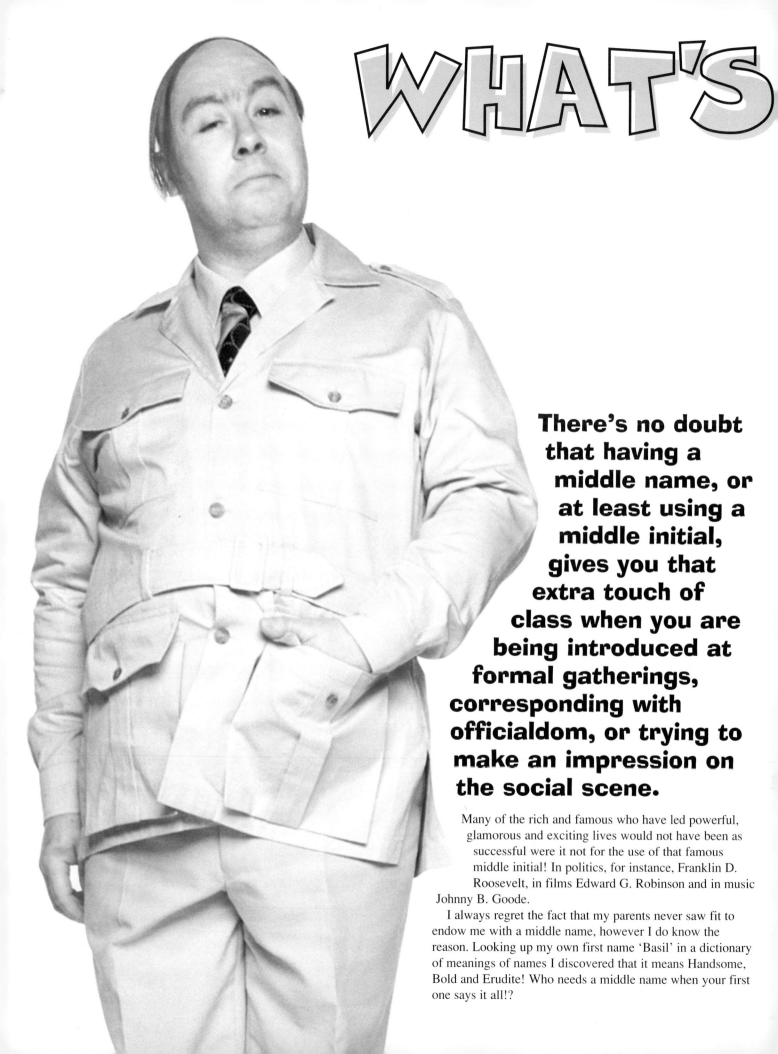

**There's no doubt that having a middle name, or at least using a middle initial, gives you that extra touch of class when you are being introduced at formal gatherings, corresponding with officialdom, or trying to make an impression on the social scene.**

Many of the rich and famous who have led powerful, glamorous and exciting lives would not have been as successful were it not for the use of that famous middle initial! In politics, for instance, Franklin D. Roosevelt, in films Edward G. Robinson and in music Johnny B. Goode.

I always regret the fact that my parents never saw fit to endow me with a middle name, however I do know the reason. Looking up my own first name 'Basil' in a dictionary of meanings of names I discovered that it means Handsome, Bold and Erudite! Who needs a middle name when your first one says it all!?

# IN A MIDDLE NAME?

If, like me, you don't require a middle name in order to make an impression, an alternative is to give yourself a number! This suggests quality and breeding as in 'Queen Elizabeth the Second' or 'George Hamilton the Fourth'. In my case, of course, it would have to be 'Basil Aldyman the One and Only.'

You could always combine the middle name with an implication of breeding. Like the poet Alfred 'Lord' Tennyson, I've often thought of calling myself Basil 'Duke' Aldyman, Basil 'Knight of The Garter' Aldyman or even Basil 'Prince' Aldyman although now that would have to be changed to Basil 'Symbol' Aldyman!

I must confess that, although I've given the matter of a middle name a great deal of thought over the years, I've never managed to settle on one I felt really added anything to my existing ones. So I thought, why not leave the choice to you! At the foot of the page I've listed my six all time favourite middle names. Simply tick the one you think is best for me and pop the cut off section in the post! The winner gets a signed photograph of Yours Truly middle name included!

Queen Elizabeth the SECOND

George Hamilton the FOURTH

Basil Aldyman the ONE AND ONLY!

---

**HORATIO** ☐

**ORSON** ☐

**TYRONE** ☐

**ALOYSIUS** ☐

**ENGELBERT** ☐

**GARY** ☐

Your Name . . . . . . . . . . . . . . . . . . . . . . . . . . . . . . . . . . . . . . . .

Your Address . . . . . . . . . . . . . . . . . . . . . . . . . . . . . . . . . . . . . . . .

. . . . . . . . . . . . . . . . . . . . . . . . . . . . . . . . . . . . . . . . . . . . . . . . . . .

. . . . . . . . . . . . . . . . . . . . . . . . . . . . . . . . . . . . . . . . . . . . . . . . . . .

. . . . . . . . . . . . . . . . . . . . . . . . . . . . . . . . . . . . . . . . . . . . . . . . . . .

Your Sex . . . . . . . . . . . . . . . . . .         Your Age . . . . . . . . . . . . . . . . . .

Signature . . . . . . . . . . . . . . . . . . . . . . . . . . . . . . . . . . . . . . . . . . . . . .

☐ Tick this box if you are not interested in receiving information about hair products.

# Four Weddings and a Funeral

**There aren't many people who can fill a suit like me, and in order to create the right impression at formal functions it's important to wear the correct attire! This means a visit to Moss Bross where you can hire a dress suit appropriate for any occasion.**

I don't know why it is but the men who wield the tape measures in Moss Bros these days seem unable to get their figures right! On the last occasion I was measured for a suit they presented me with a most unflattering set of vital statistics telling me they were my personal measurements! Of course I knew they couldn't be and insisted they change their figures to the correct ones. They then compounded their error by supplying me with a suit I was unable to get into!

Because of this I was forced to put on a pair of pink crushed denim dungarees (with a zip pocket across the chest) a yellow shirt and a purple cummerbund and attend the occasion wearing that. Fortunately the family of the man whose funeral it was were very understanding.

# GET ME TO THE CHURCH ON TIME!

Yes, 'Get Me To The Church On Time!' as the old song goes! I always attend several weddings during the course of the year, although this can be difficult, mainly because I haven't been invited. This is obviously an oversight on the part of the person sending out the invitations so if it's family, friend, colleague or even a complete stranger who's getting married I'll go along anyway.

It pays to get into Church early and get a good seat. I usually park myself down on the front pew in order to be close enough to act as prompt to the young couple should they forget their lines – or, if the Mother-In-Law looks a bit of a dragon, to try and get the Groom to change his mind before it's too late. A word of warning here. Someone called an "Usher" may come and ask you to move to another seat. Ignore him. These so called "Ushers" have no legal powers whatsoever!

If you don't like the choice of hymns, **say so**. If they refuse to change them, write down a list of **your** selection and circulate this to the guests. Even if the bride's family refuses your request to take a vote on which hymns

to have – yours or theirs – you will at least have shown the assembled congregation that you have a superior taste in music! Finally, refuse to sing along.

# A DAY TO REMEMBER

After the ceremony everyone will troop outside to have their picture taken. There will be an official 'photographer' there – give him a chance, but in all probability you will have to take over. In photographs composition is everything. Get a family group together and make sure the Groom is right in the centre. Then when you're happy that the picture is ready to be taken, get the Groom to come out and operate the camera while you take his place. This will ensure the bride has a wonderful reminder of her perfect day!

*This chap looks like he could do with a hand!*

# A SENSE OF DIRECTION

## How many times have you been stopped in the street by a complete stranger asking for directions?

I must admit for some reason it doesn't often happen to me, but if I see someone else trying to give directions I will always go over to help. Usually the person giving the directions will have no idea what he's talking about so naturally I have to take over. The lost stranger will often become so confident of his bearings after a few moments of instruction from me that he will begin to set off down the streeet of his own accord!

Many people, when asked to provide directions, will resort to having to draw a map. This is time-consuming, the end result can be confusing and also have the effect of completely ruining the back of the envelope you were about to post. Take my advice. Do as I do and always carry several copies of an already prepared map with all the major landmarks clearly marked! You will be surprised at how many of these you have to hand out in a normal day – especially if you stand right in front of the public display board Town Map.

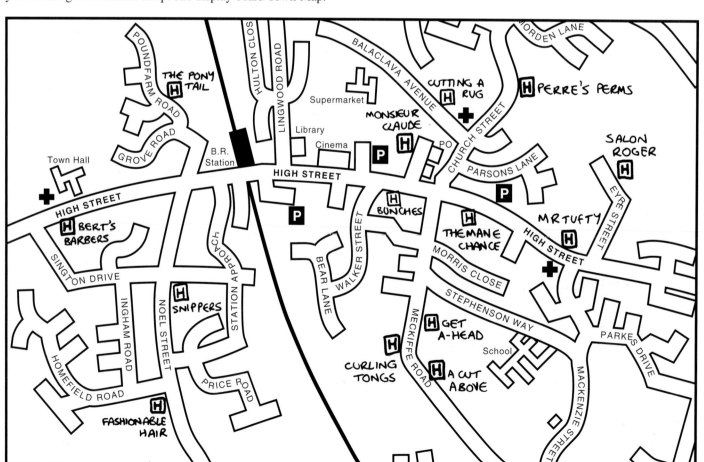

# CAUGHT BY THE TABLOIDS!

Being someone other people naturally want to read about can have its drawbacks. Both Princess Diana and myself have suffered at the hands of a seemingly insatiable media. I too know what it's like to have the paparazzi constantly camped on one's doorstep; to know there are hidden photographers with telephoto lenses trying to snap you in unflattering poses (impossible in my case!); and to receive constant requests to appear in lifestyle articles for 'HELLO' magazine!

So how do you restrict the demands of the press without giving the impression you're publicity shy? For a happy relationship with the media the answer is to make yourself available at pre-arranged times - major events in your life, for instance - but also to let them snap you in your spicier moments!

## Thousands gather to see Pavarotti in the Park

ME!

A quiet night out at a concert is captured by a press photographer, though fortunately he'd forgotten his telephoto lens!

The joy of my birth is turned into a media circus!

**Births:**
Aldyman. Mr and Mrs Aldyman are delighted to announce the birth of a son, Basil.

I allow my birthday to become an annual excuse for the press to tell the world the secret of my success

**TAURUS** (April 21 – May 21) Your natural charm, easy style and good looks bring great rewards.

It's good to let the Society pages have a glimpse of your love life

## ☎ *Romance Line*

**Young, slim, athletic** and hirsuit entrepreneur (own mobile phone) seeks partner for fun nights of train-spotting and crosswords. Please supply stamp so I can send you my photo.

The press were delighted when I allowed nude photos of me to be splashed across the front pages! P.T.O.

**Estd. 1972**

Current circulation: 1,706.

Issue number: 1209

Weekly publication

# THE RUGWICH RECORDER

# CONFIDENTIAL MEDICAL RECORDS FOUND ON TIP!

**Red-faced hospital chiefs say they have no idea how the medical records of Mr. B. Aldyman came to be found on a local rubbish tip.**

The confidential records of the extensive medical history of Mr. Aldyman of Axminster Avenue, Rugwich, were found yesterday morning by sanitary worker Ken Harbottle, who promptly handed the documents over to the police. Mr. Aldyman's doctor is helping the police with their enquiries, after it was discovered the doctor had written "This man is a total hypochondriac. Get rid of him!" on the front of the file. **Full story page 6**

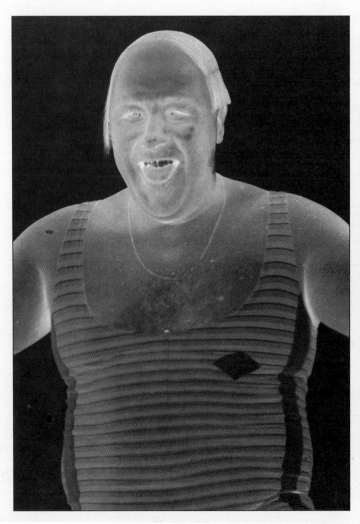
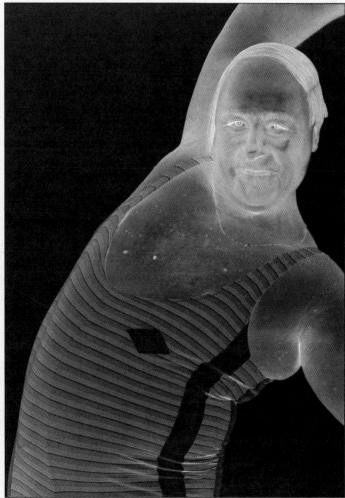

# WORK THAT BODY

A healthy body means a healthy mind - and a fine healthy head of hair! Today exercise pro-grammes have become big business thanks to the antics of keep fit gurus such as Mr Motivator on Breakfast Television.

Get In, Shape Up, Look Out and Dance
with
**MR HUNKIVATOR!**

WORK THAT BODY

If, like me, you're extremely fit, healthy and very active – but don't get up in time to see Mr Motivator in the mornings – then what you need is my own specially made Exercise Video!

This is simply **THE NEW BEST SELLING EXERCISE VIDEO FOR MEN!** Of course women will buy it too, ostensibly for their husbands but really so they can secretly watch and admire my panther-like figure going through its macho routine.

**The MR HUNKIVATOR Exercise Programme couldn't be easier!**

## Step One

Get the video out of the box! Pop it into the video recorder! Grab the remote and press play! By now you should have worked up quite a sweat!

## Step Two

Before embarking on the keep fit routine itself, it's advisable to perform a few simple limbering up exercises. These are quite different to the physical jerks themselves.

▲ **A Limbering Up Exercrise**

◀ **A Physical Jerk**

# Step **Three**

Once you've limbered up it's time to start on the exercises proper, so pump up the volume and start working that body to some of the best music around.

▶ **If I Said You Had A Beautiful Body Would You Hold It Against Me**

▼ **Do Ya Think I'm Sexy**

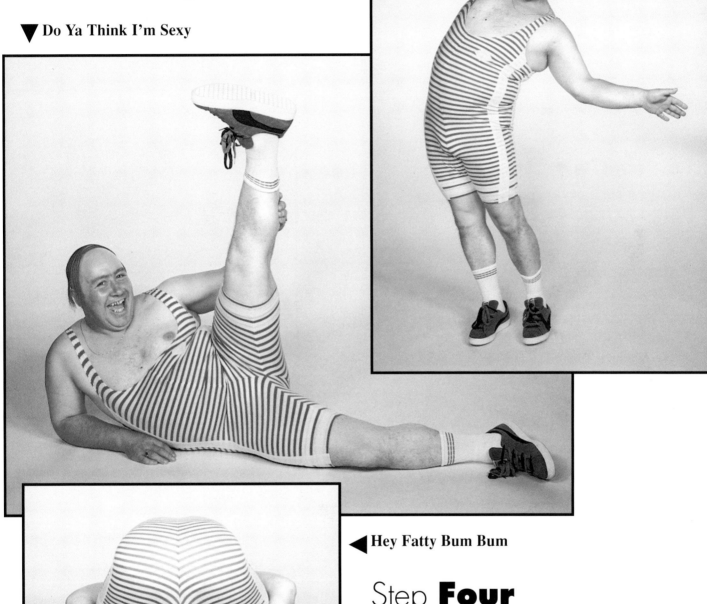

◀ **Hey Fatty Bum Bum**

# Step **Four**

Most exercise videos are for you to use in the privacy of your own home, Not the **MR HUNKIVATOR** exercise programme. You want to show off your new physique so start by throwing back the curtains, opening the blinds and working out in your lounge window. As you gain more confidence you will want to exercise in the front garden, watching the video through the window. This never fails to collect an admiring crowd and you will be the talk of street!

# Step **Five**

Having mastered the basic body movements necessary to keep yourself in trim, you might want to try out some of the simple exercise equipment available for home use. Towards the end of the video I demonstrate the correct – and safe – way to get the best out of this gadgetry!

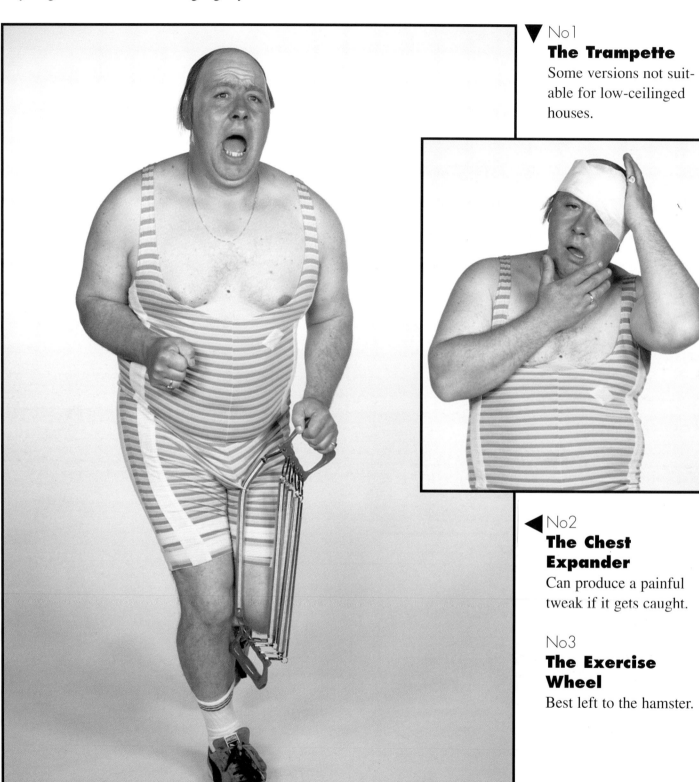

▼ No1
## **The Trampette**
Some versions not suitable for low-ceilinged houses.

◄ No2
## **The Chest Expander**
Can produce a painful tweak if it gets caught.

No3
## **The Exercise Wheel**
Best left to the hamster.

# Spring, when a Baldyman's fancy turns to love

| | | | MARCH | | | |
|---|---|---|---|---|---|---|
| M | T | W | T | F | S | S |
| | | | | 1 | **2** | **3** |
| 4 | 5 | 6 | 7 | 8 | **9** | **10** |
| 11 | 12 | 13 | 14 | 15 | **16** | **17** |
| 18 | 19 | 20 | 21 | 22 | **23** | **24** |
| 25 | 26 | 27 | 28 | 29 | **30** | **31** |

| | | | APRIL | | | |
|---|---|---|---|---|---|---|
| M | T | W | T | F | S | S |
| 1 | 2 | 3 | 4 | 5 | **6** | **7** |
| 8 | 9 | 10 | 11 | 12 | **13** | **14** |
| 15 | 16 | 17 | 18 | 19 | **20** | **21** |
| 22 | 23 | 24 | 25 | 26 | **27** | **28** |
| 29 | 30 | | | | | |

# MAKE YOUR WAY IN THE WORLD WITH MY PERSONALLY DESIGNED
# SOCIAL LADDER

|  |  |
|------|------|
| 1996 | LIFE PEER |
| 1993 | KNIGHTHOOD |
| 1990 | INVITATION TO ROYAL GARDEN PARTY |
| 1988 | FAMOUS DOCTOR/WRITER/SCIENTIST |
| 1982 | KISS JOANNA LUMLEY |
| 1978 | PLAY FOOTBALL FOR ENGLAND |
| 1974 | PERM |
| 1973 | SECOND SHAVE |
| 1972 | FIRST SHAVE |
| 1971 | SCHOOL PREFECT |
| 1969 | SCOUTS GOLD ARROW |
| 1966 | CYCLING PROFICIENCY TEST |
| 1965 | LONG TROUSERS |
| 1962 | WOLF CUBS FIRE LIGHTING BADGE |
| 1960 | CLOAK ROOM MONITOR |
| 1957 | NAPPY TRAINED |

Simply set yourself goals and tick off each one as it is achieved.

I drew up my own ladder several years ago and I confess I am a little behind schedule, but because I have planned ahead I am confident of my eventual total success!

# PARTY GIVER EXTRAORDINAIRE

**Every now and then I fell the need to reward my friends and acquaintances by giving them the chance to enjoy themselves in my company. You should do the same. But be warned, a meagre get together is no use at all! The mother of all parties should involve anything up to seven or eight people! This is exactly the right number for treading that treacherous tightrope between controlled cordiality and reckless mayhem!**

## THE INVITATIONS

Let's start with the invitations. Timing is a vital element. You must always give people plenty of notice of a party. It never ceases to amaze me how many of my acquaintances, when told about my "swinging soiree", turn out to have pressing prior engagements. Because of this I always try to get my invitations out six months in advance, although even then two people were unable to come to my last 'do' – one citing a clash with his grandmother's funeral and the other insisting he had to stay in and wash his hair (the second excuse quite understandable, of course!)

Spend some time drawing up a guest list. One of my old ones is shown below to give you some ideas.

GUEST LIST FOR MY PARTY

females

Claudia Schiffer
Elle Macpherson
Cindy Crawford
Dame Kiri Te Kanawa
Raquel from Coronation St.
Virginia Bottomley
Betty Boothroyd

Males

Capt. Jean Luc Picard
Right Said Fred
Duncan Goodhew
Uncle Fester

Always get your invitations professionally made up. There's nothing I enjoy more than walking into a printers, telling them I'm having a party and ordering 500 invitations! That's what I call creating an impression! (Besides it's always wise to send out a few extra just in case 490 people don't turn up.) If you're not sure what to put on the invitations here's a copy of one of my best efforts!

### MR. B.ALDYMAN, ESQ.

*Cordially invites you and*
*THREE FEMALE FRIENDS*
*of your choice to his*

### SUMMER SOIREE

**Bring three bottles**

**Entry by cash**

**Be there or have corners!**

## THE BIG DAY

On the big day itself be sure to lock away all your valuables. Having them locked away means that you then have to describe to your guests what your wide screen TV looks like, how versatile your top of the range PC is and the exquisite shape and colour of your Ming vase. Not that your living room should be totally bare for the function. I find the careful positioning of two or

three lava lamps, the addition of beaded curtains between the lounge and dining area (where the refreshments will be) and – the piece de resistance – a glitterball for the dancing, is all you need to turn your pad into Party Central! (Oh, and don't forget to leave out a couple of thermometers to guage the Night Fever!)

# MUSIC

Without music your party will be like Tarzan without vines, it simply won't swing! So get out the gramaphone, put the needle on the vinyl, crank the dial right up to five or six and to heck with the neighbours! (Review this situation after half past nine on a week night.) Sometimes people can be reluctant to get up and dance but with my choice of music I guarantee there won't be an occupied seat in the room! Here's a suggested 'playlist' for getting the joint swinging!

| | |
|---|---|
| **THE BLUEBELL POLKA** | **Jimmy Shand and his Band** |
| **D.I.S.C.O.** | **Ottowan** |
| **B.A.L.D.Y.** | **Phil Collins** |
| **TWO LITTLE BOYS** | **Rolf Harris** |
| **ROCK THE NIGHT AWAY** | **Val Doonican** |

# THE PERFECT HOST

As the perfect host you will be expected to mingle. My guests always seem to respect this and are often only too happy for me to move on and chat to someone else. When you've spoken to everybody at least once, the ice should be broken sufficiently for you to bring out the PARTY GAMES!

# PARTY GAMES

This is the high spot of the evening for my guests, especially Postman's Knock where some lucky female gets to kiss yours truly! Unfortunately the excitement has often proved too much for the lady in question who has either choked violently on a twiglet, fainted or locked herself in the bathroom before I have even puckered my lips. My advice is to START with 'Postman's Knock', (before the small talk, the drinks and the music) or else hide the nibbles, keep the room temperature low and tell everyone the bathroom's out of order.

If the excitement of 'Postman's Knock' should prove too much, a good game to move onto is 'Hide and Seek'. This has always proved a great success at my parties and it's funny how I'm always chosen as the first person to hide. Often it can take the rest of the evening for the guests to find me. In fact on one occasion I emerged from my hiding place to discover the house was completely empty! Everyone thought I'd actually left the house and gone to THEIR homes, as that's where they went to look for me! We had a good laugh about that and I told them I'd get my own back when I visited their homes – strangely enough I haven't yet been invited.

# MAKING A WRITTEN IMPRESSION

**The pen is mightier than the sword, although not unfortunately mightier than the rolled up umbrella as I discovered during a misunderstanding with a little old lady over a parking space last Saturday afternoon.**

**But if you want to make a real impression don't let others walk over you.
COMPLAIN!**

Basil Aldyman Esq.
"Duncombin"
Axminster Avenue
Rugwich

Mr Mohammed Al Fayed
Chairman
Harrods
Knightsbridge
London

Dear Sir,

I wish to protest in the strongest possible terms about my treatment by one of your doormen last week for refusing me admission to your shop on the grounds that I was breaching your "dress code". I was not wearing ripped jeans, a PVC thong or some other such unsuitable attire and therefore asked him to explain what the matter was, whereupon he ventured that I "looked ridiculous".

I don't know how long you and your brother have been in the retail trade but I presume you have heard the expression "the customer is always right". On that basis, if I want to look ridiculous then I jolly well shall and for that matter I have looked ridiculous in better places than your jumped up penny arcade.

Yours "ridiculously",

*Basil Aldyman*

Basil Aldyman Esquire

Miss A. Chamberlain
Artistic Director
Rugwich Community Theatre

Basil Aldyman Esq.
"Duncombin"
Axminster Avenue
Rugwich

Dear Miss Chamberlain,

NO! I would not like to play Humpty Dumpty in this years pantomime. I find your request both offensive and impertinent.

Not Yours EVER!,

*Basil Aldyman*

Basil Aldyman

Customer Relations Officer
Baldigon Hair Growth Accelerator
PO Box 11
Glasgow

**Basil Aldyman Esq.**
**"Duncombin"**
**Axminster Avenue**
**Rugwich**

A friend of mine recently purchased a bottle of your accelerator by mail order, a friend who incidentally suffers the indignity of premature hair loss. Far from delivering the promised lush re-growth, your product removed the top three layers of skin from my friend's scalp and caused the appearance of scarlet welts — making him look not unlike Noel Edmonds' comical partner "Mr Blobby". Furthermore it still stings like crazy. Or so he tells me. My friend, that is.
People like you who prey on the unfortunate deserve all you get and you may be interested to know that the stinging sensation in your fingers derives from the fact that I have soaked this letter in your potion. So you'll have some idea how ~~my friend's~~ my friend's head feels.!

Yours in revenge,

*Basil Aldyman*

Basil Aldyman

**Basil Aldyman Esq.**
**"Duncombin"**
**Axminster Avenue**
**Rugwich**

The Producer
Darts Related Quiz Show Prgramming
Northern Television
Lancs.

Dear Sir,
I notice from your very clever quiz show that to be a contestant on your Darts Quiz Show you must be over fifteen stone with at least three chins and two bellies, one on top of the other. But so much for the women, what I really want to know is how does a man like myself get a chance at Mr Bull's Prize Board and ultimately the Star Prize?
I am aware of the basic principals of dartology and am very good at quiz shows (I'm sick of always winning "Childs Play"!) and I promise to laugh at all of the presenter's jokes. Even the two-handers with the little fat bloke who says, "iiiiinnn one, iiiiiiinnnn two," etc, etc.
So come on Mr Producer, do the ratings a favour and give a suave goodlooker like myself a shot at Mr Bull!

Yours showbusinessly,

*Basil Aldyman*

Basil Aldyman

Mr Terry Wogan
BBC TV
London

**Basil Aldyman Esq.**
**"Duncombin"**
**Axminster Avenue**
**Rugwich**

Dear Mr Wogan,
Recently your hair weave seems to have slipped through 30 degrees.

Get a life!  Don't you realise how ridiculous you look.

A friend.

# BASIL ALDYMAN

## THE DANDY OF OUR TV SCREENS LETS US HAVE A DEKKO AT HIS DECOR!

**O**n entering this swank, singular semi, the first things you notice are the cork ceiling tiles, the hessian wallpaper and the preponderance of Artex – even on the doors. Standing proudly in the doorway Basil admits it's taken him fifteen years to get the house into its present state, but it's been worth it. On a recent visit a local estate agent confirmed that all the work he had done had certainly had a profound effect on the value of the property… which had plummeted by 90%.

A great collector of ornaments Basil admits the chess set (pictured left) is purely for display. Not that he doesn't enjoy the mental stimulation of a challenging game of wits. "I'm a Kerplunk man!" says he loftily. And you can bet your bottom dollar that when a Kerplunk set made of imitation pink marble with a mirrored base comes on the market he'll be the first to buy one!

Another outstanding feature in the lounge is an adjustable suspended light shade made with fake tiger skin (which matches the cover on the sofa) stretched over a heavy brass frame. This impressive fitment can be raised or lowered as required and certainly is worthy of the term 'stunning'. In fact our photographer was stunned for several minutes after striking his head against it.

In the kitchen Basil revealed that mending, washing and ironing were no problem to this resourceful bachelor! He simply takes it all round to his mother and gets her to do it. Not that he isn't a dab hand with the Morphy Richards when the occasion demands! We caught him ironing a designer label fashion apron prior to tackling a bit of hoovering. "I don't know why it is," Basil complained as he got the Hoover Dustette out if its box under the sink, "but falling hair and dandruff seem to get everywhere!"

For someone who's so fastidious about keeping his house clean we weren't surprised to discover that Basil is obsessive about personal

hygiene too. The small 8cm by 5cm white plastic sign, bought in a souvenir shop in Morecambe and glued to the bathroom door says it all – 'Basil's Bathroom'.

Inside the cabinet shelves were groaning with shampoo and aftershave – particular favourites being 'Hunk', 'Stud', 'He-Man', 'Stallion' and 'Old Spice Lime'. Ornaments were in evidence too. Basil proudly showed us a china bowl positioned exactly in the centre of the bathroom windowsill especially to catch the clippings when he's cutting his toenails. "It keeps them off the floor and they make an interesting addition to the pot-pourri." he explained.

Of all the rooms in the house the bedroom is the one Basil admits he feels most at home in. "I think it's because of the mirrors" he says, one of which looks like it comes from a film star's dressing room and is surrounded by a border of twenty light bulbs. "Originally they were 60 watt bulbs, but I had to have them replaced by 100 watt ones." Basil explains. " My smile was just too bright for the 60 watts!"

Finally, how does Basil choose his interior decor? "Anything subtle, understated and tasteful is okay with me" he says. "At home I like to feel comfortable by blending in with my surroundings."

**No need to get steamed up with the steam iron! The Man About Town (above left) shows us he can be a Man About The House too! (Above) Basil's Bathroom! Basil confesses there's nothing he enjoys more than a good long soak – and he likes to sing in the tub too! Usually he warbles a bit of light opera, his particular favourite is the 'Barber of Seville'. (Below) Basil blends in!**

**A distressing thought sometimes crosses my mind. The fact that there is a limit to the number of people you can impress. Once you have stamped your identity on your neighbourhood, become well known to officialdom in your own country and have travelled abroad to bestow your superior knowledge and attitudes on those living in foreign countries, what further challenge is there?**

**The answer is  The Challenge of Outer Space!**

## U.F.O. CLUBS

When I first became interested in the subject of life on other planets, I naturally joined my local Flying Saucer Enthusiasts Club, going with them on several 'Saucer Spotting' weekends. Strangely enough shortly after I joined many of their members reported seeing a small, shiny, pinkish dome like object hovering about. I never saw it and was forced to conclude that most members of the club had highly suspect eyesight or overdeveloped imaginations!

I handed in my resignation and wrote a strongly worded letter to the Flying Saucer Clubs official regulator OffUFO. The message was simply 'OffU**GO** OffUFO' which I felt was clever, apt & amusing in the circumstances.

The simple truth of the matter is that if Aliens want to get in touch they will find a way! So in order to create the right impression when they do you must be prepared!

## WHAT TO DO WHEN CONFRONTED WITH AN ALIEN?

The standard opening gambit for an alien being is 'Take me to your Leader!' This, of course, will not apply in my case as the alien will instantly recognise me as being of a superior quality to my fellow men, and has in fact probably singled me out for this very reason.

The Alien will almost certainly have a vital message from his planet intended for your ears alone. You must get him into your house as quickly as possible. This will serve the dual purpose of keeping him away from media attention and showing him what good taste you have in interior design. (Incidentally there have been stories of Aliens carting human beings away and removing their vital organs. Just as a precaution as soon as you get back to the house the first thing you should do is hide all your donor cards.)

# PHONE ME!

## COMMUNICATING

If the Alien cannot speak English it will be up to you find a way of communicating with him. If questions like 'Parlez-Vous Klingon?' elicit no response then play him the theme from 'Close Encounters of the Third Kind' on your stylophone. If he shows interest in the stylophone then you've cracked it like you, he's a Technophile! Show him your Desk Top Calculator, your Breville

Sandwich Toaster and especially your Betamax Video Recorder, as he may be able to tell you where you can get tapes for it.

## SMALL TALK

Once communication has been established make him feel at ease by indulging in some informal small talk, but remember he's from another planet not from next door!

### THINGS YOU CAN SAY TO ALIENS YOU CANNOT SAY TO YOUR NEXT DOOR NEIGHBOUR

1) **Come upstairs and I'll show you my telescope.**

2) **I noticed that huge pus-filled gangrenous spot on your nose right away!***

3) **Yes I did vote Tory.**

* (NB. No.2. This is a good way of letting the Alien know that you feel comfortable with his appearance, no matter what it is. Don't forget they may find **our** looks distasteful! In my own case I'm aware that many Aliens are smooth headed and may be terrified by my luxurious full sweep of hair!)

# DOWN TO BUSINESS

Once the ice has been broken it'll be down to business. The Alien will be curious. He will want to know where he can see the prime examples of the human species at work, at play, at home and abroad. This is an opportunity the like of which you have never had before and which you may never have again. Do not waste it! Grasp it firmly with both hands! GET YOUR PHOTO-GRAPH ALBUMS OUT!

Many humans captured by Aliens have described how they lost track of time. How several hours seemed to flash past in a second. This is what it will be like for the Alien as I show him my photo albums full of pictures of me from the year dot to the present day! If Aliens required proof of the existence of highly intelligent, advanced, sophisticated life forms on Earth it is all there in black & white, and from 1959 in colour too!

If any further proof is needed, pictures of yourself with world leaders should be produced. Fortunately I have many of these in my 'Celebrity Photo Album'.

## BEAM ME UP, SCOTTY!

The time will come for the Alien to take his leave. Quickly turning down your offer to introduce him to other earthlings he will 'beam up' to his space ship and disappear faster than the speed of light. But contact will have been made. Keep watching the skies!

# SIX SIMPLE WAYS TO BECOME
# FAMOUS!

**1.**
Discover a new comet.

**2.**
Win Mastermind.

**3.**
Achieve a breakthrough in medicine.

**4.**
Have an item of clothing named after you.

**5.**
Find a new continent.

**6.**
Be seen with Joanna Lumley.

# GOING MOBILE

If, like me, you're the kind of cool dude who likes to keep in touch even when he's on the move, then a mobile phone is a vital accessory. It says something about you – 'Here's a guy who's popular, important and SERIOUSLY IN DEMAND!'

## CHOOSING A MOBILE

Always pick a phone shop with a large display window, then you can check out your reflection as you try the different sets. Closed circuit TV security monitors are good for this too though they do tend to show you from above and can give the totally wrong impression that you have a bald patch!

Many salesmen will tell you that in choosing a mobile phone you've got to get the right profile. This is completely wrong. In my case the left profile is just as stunning.

## ON THE ROAD

You can use a mobile phone whilst driving but if you do this, to be absolutely safe, always STOP THE CAR. Ignore the other traffic behind you. A good place to do this is in the middle of single lane roadworks. Initially the drivers behind will honk their horns and flash their lights but if you wave and point to indicate that you're taking an important phone call they'll soon understand the kind of person you are! Having a phone in the car is also useful because it enables you to quickly report **other** motorists' bad driving!

## ON THE TOWN

Say you've gone to the theatre and you've left the car at home. Coming to the end of the performance you'll be thinking of calling for a taxi. Once the curtain comes down everyone will be wanting one so don't wait till the last minute. Pick a quiet moment in the performance – a love scene or a death scene – then, as you're booking your cab, you won't have to struggle to make yourself heard above the actors!

## BE WARNED

Mobile phones can be faulty! I had to return my handset after 2 weeks because it hadn't received any incoming calls at all! B.T. tried to suggest this might be because no one had telephoned me. I of course scoffed at this. I also took the opportunity to point out that their chatline service was out of order. Several times I'd called it up and found no one wanting to chat!

# One of the most evocative sounds of summer – the crack of leather against wood

## MAY

| M | T | W | T | F | S | S |
|---|---|---|---|---|---|---|
| | | 1 | 2 | 3 | 4 | 5 |
| 6 | 7 | 8 | 9 | 10 | 11 | 12 |
| 13 | 14 | 15 | 16 | 17 | 18 | 19 |
| 20 | 21 | 22 | 23 | 24 | 25 | 26 |
| 27 | 28 | 29 | 30 | 31 | | |

## JUNE

| M | T | W | T | F | S | S |
|---|---|---|---|---|---|---|
| | | | | | 1 | 2 |
| 3 | 4 | 5 | 6 | 7 | 8 | 9 |
| 10 | 11 | 12 | 13 | 14 | 15 | 16 |
| 17 | 18 | 19 | 20 | 21 | 22 | 23 |
| 24 | 25 | 26 | 27 | 28 | 29 | 30 |

# Acquire Superior Skills

**TAKE UP THAT DANGEROUS SPORT**

Women are impressed by men who dice with danger! I myself am no stranger to 'life on the edge'. I have often not returned a library book till five minutes before the library closed on the day it was due back! And I still get cold shivers up & down my spine when I think of the day I came through the '9 items or less 'checkout at the supermarket with **10 items**!

But nothing impresses a female more than a man who takes part in a dangerous sport. They are attracted to these males like bees round a honeypot, one only has to count the number of 'hangers-on' at the hang gliding club! I myself was once pestered for several months by some table-tennis groupies.

Simply, any sport which has the whiff of excitement about it will pull in the ladies and the one I've chosen to instruct you in is windsurfing! There's certainly a whiff about wind!

Unlike many sports you don't have to spend a lot of money buying equipment in order to become a windsurfer. All you need is an ironing board, some string, and an old sheet.

Simply tie these to the roof of your car and drive about holiday picnic spots and beach car parks and you'll instantly become recognised as one of the windsurfing set! It helps if you always wear a waterproof watch as somebody **may** ask you the time. If nobody does then go up to somebody and ask **them** the time ostentatiously tapping your watch as they tell you.

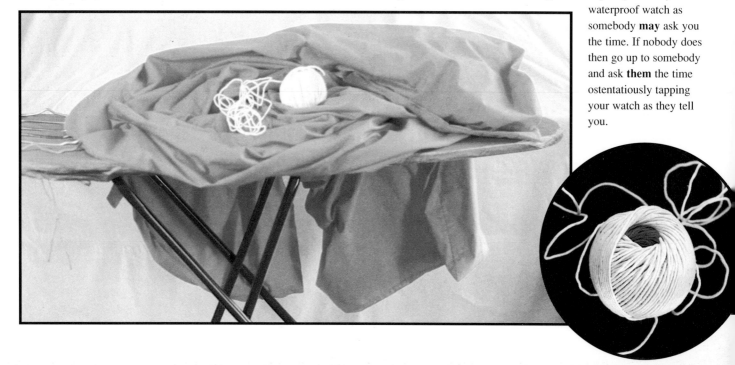

# GETTING STARTED

As with any new activity practice makes perfect! You can teach yourself the first basic steps of windsurfing, such as balance and holding the string, quite easily in the home by following my simple step by step instructions.

1) **Stand on the ironing board in a crouching position and spread your weight evenly through your body.**
2) **Slowly stand up.**
3) **Bang head on ceiling.**
4) **Remove ironing board legs.**
5) **Repeat steps 1 & 2.**

After you've learned to stand on the ironing board it's time to practice holding the sheet! For this, of course, you need some wind. Obviously to create the necessary force 5 or 6 gale in your own home you'd have to have about 100 hairdriers which is ridiculous! Fortunately I have 73 hairdriers which is enough to generate a fairly stiff breeze. An added advantage is by having them all set to 'warm' I can give the effect of windsurfing in the Caribbean.

# ON THE WATER

Once you've got accustomed to stance & balance in the home, it's time to try your 'board' out on the water. You may not live near the sea or have a large area of inland water near you but don't worry. Simply pop along to your local swimming baths and enquire which night is windsurfers' night. Make it clear that you are a serious windsurfer who wishes to go up and down the length of the pool and you don't want to go on a night when the more frivolous windsurfers are allowed in to do 'widths'. If your local baths doesn't have a windsurfers' night, which in my experience is more than likely, complain loudly. (Ignore any comments they make about hot air coming from your direction – jealousy about your new skill will have already set in!)

# THE REAL THING

At last your chance to show off your talents at the seaside! Don't head for the water right away. It pays to mingle with the windsurfing set first. You will find they are a friendly bunch, happy to compare watches, talk about Chris Rea CDs and share a can of 'Lilt' with you. This initial camaraderie can quickly turn nasty, however, if, after you explain that your board is still tied to the roof of your car, one of them offers to 'let you have a go on his board!' This is dangerous territory. Often they have boards made to individual specifications – lethal and terrifying **'One Man Boards'** – which can tip another windsurfer, no matter how experienced, into the water making you look foolish in front of the women.

The way to deal with this is to politely decline, say you've pulled a muscle and affect a limp as you leave. Head straight back home. You will have made an impression as part of the hunky dangerous sport set and you'll probably find there is some ironing to do.

# SOAP GETS IN YOUR EYES

## A GUIDE TO THE BEST SHAMPOOS

**What do you hear when you open a bottle of shampoo ? Most people would say 'FUTT! SQUIRT!', but not me! I hear peals of bells, the crashing of waves on the ocean, brass bands and heavenly choirs and occasionally Captain Sensible singing 'Happy Talk'.**

**Opening a bottle of shampoo should be almost a spiritual experience. You unscrew the top, flick open the cap and for the first time breathe in the intoxicating heady aroma of 'fern', 'raspberry' or 'toad-in-the-hole'. In a moment you know the delicately fragranced liquid presently captivated in that bottle will cascade over your head making every follicle tingle. There is no more enjoyable experience first thing in the morning than having tingling follicles.**

**As a Connoisseur of Cranial Cleanliness with years of shampoo use behind me - and ahead of me - let me guide you through the maze of products currently on the market.**

### SHAMPOO SEARCH

Every bottle of shampoo is different. They can vary enormously depending on their place of origin. From the crisp, lemony whites of 'Boots' to the deep mysterious reds of the 'Body Shop'. Some shampoos are best used at once, others benefit from being 'laid down' (normally at the back of the bathroom cabinet where you only discover them again when you're looking for the eyebath.)

**Aloe Vera & Cucumber for Frequent Use.**
A nice everyday shampoo. Light and bubbly with a good foamy finish. Great fun for when I'm showering with one of my friends - Billy Backbrush, Simon Sponge or Larry the Loofah.

**Peach & Melon with Kiwi, Pear, Raspberry, Cherry, Tangerine, Gooseberry, Mango and Banana.**
Surprisingly fruity. Should be pinkish in colour. If you get a bottle which is blue it's likely that something has gone badly wrong some-where in the process, probably at the labell-ing stage.

**Organic Balsam.**
Produced from organically grown Balsams and therefore environmentally friendly. This shampoo is specially formulated to nourish your roots and is smooth on the pate with a lingering bouquet of natural fertilisers. One for enjoying alone on those increasingly regular long evenings spent washing your hair.

**Milky Bar and Spearmint for Blondes.**
Blondes have more fun, they say, and it's certainly true with this cheeky little number. Whether you're ash blonde, platinum blonde or strawberry blonde like me this is the shampoo for you! (Also available in Creme Egg & Rolo for Redheads, Egg Mayonaise for Slapheads and Bio-Medicated with Essence of Elastoplast for blackheads.)

**Special Formula Triple X for thinning hair.**
Never tried it.

Finally, if you find yourself having to wash your hair in a hotel and not sure which shampoo to use you're usually safe with a bottle of the **House Vosene.**

# So!! Are You A
# GO-GETTER?

## (Or a Not-Got-It!?)

### I have devised this quiz that reveals the 'Real' YOU at work!

**1** The 'Boss' is about to use the photo-copier but it's broken, do you...

**a** Tell him you have phoned the engineer

**b** Blame a colleague for breaking it and point at him

**c** Try to retrieve your tie quietly from inside the machinery

**2** Your Boss has given you an important report to put the finishing touches to, do you...

**a** Do it straight away

**b** Do it when you can be bothered

**c** Give it to someone else as you are not very good at stapling

**3** The Boss is obviously jealous of your new red trousers, do you...

**a** Stop wearing them

**b** Take them off before he sees them

**c** Get mummy to knit him a pair as well

**4** Someone is collecting for a colleague going on maternity leave, do you...

**a** Give generously

**b** Refuse to donate

**c** Donate but only on condition that you get a receipt and that the child is named after you

**5** A FAX arrives addressed to you, do you...

**a** Accidently drop it on everyone's desk on the way back

**b** Leave it in the machine until the Boss sees it

**c** Act nonchalant and discreetly have it framed and hung beside the other one.

**6** Your Boss is having a party at his house to which you have been invited, do you...

**a** Say you have another appointment

**b** Say that you never mix business with pleasure

**c** Go, but refuse to smile as you move around the room with a tray of drinks to be served

## SO HOW DID YOU SCORE?

**Mainly A**
Get a life! What a loser.

**Mainly B**
Some signs that you could be as successful as ME!

**Mainly C**
What a Whizz Kid!! Wow, like myself you know how to get on. Indeed my boss said only yesterday that if he goes I will get his job. I remember his exact words "You'll get this job over my dead body."

# MODELLING MADE EASY!

With my dark, brooding good looks, perfect bone structure and slim, almost sinewy, build you'd think I'd be up there with Europe's top male models, swaggering sensuously down the catwalks of Milan & Paris. Sadly I'm just an inch too short.

If Mother Nature sold you short on the height front too (though in my case she more than made up for it in other areas!) don't despair. There are plenty of other openings for male models where square-jawed, yet sensitive, good looks - rather than an excess of inches - are the main requirement.

**REMEMBER**, somebody has to be the moussed hair, Kenneth Branagh look-a-like in the Armani advert; somebody has to pose as the dangerous, designer stubbled macho man in the Versace promotion; and somebody has to be the thoughtful chisel-cheeked stranger on the scratch 'n' sniff aftershave pages! It's all down to creating the right image, and after only ten years of circulating a portfolio of pictures of myself to every modelling agency in the U.K. my looks finally did the trick! I was snapped up and have been in constant employment since.

Here are just a few of the advertising campaigns you might remember me from!

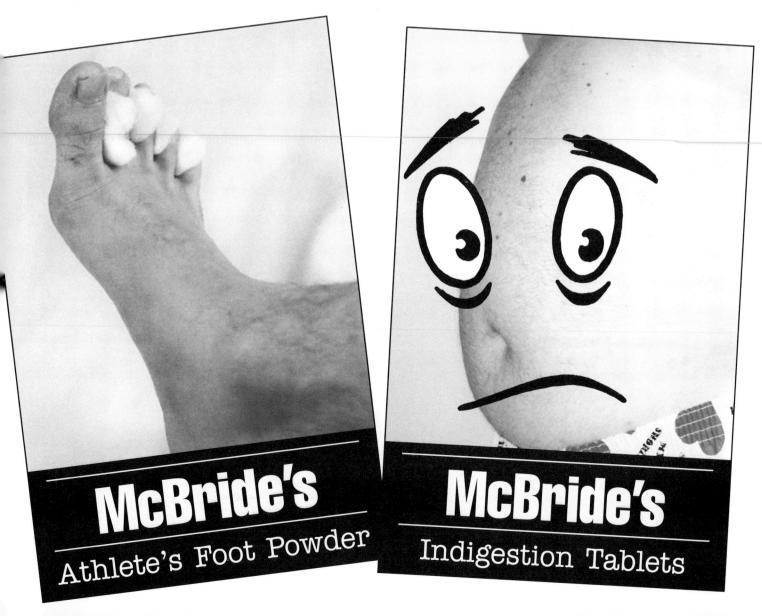

McBride's Athlete's Foot Powder

McBride's Indigestion Tablets

# LIGHTS! CAMERA! ACTION!

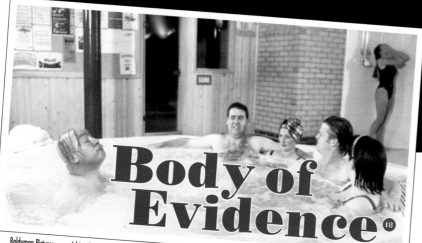

## Body of Evidence 18

Baldyman Pictures presents an Adrian Sington production a Jake Lingwood film starring B.Aldyman in Body Of Evidence co-producer Humphrey Price music by Electric Light Orchestra edited by Clare Hulton production designer Christine Corton director of photography Chantal Noel based on the novel by Grianne Ashton costumes designed by Jean-Paul Gaultier produced by Karen Ellison Vicky Johnson Katy Carrington Vicky Monk directed by Jake Lingwood screenplay by Julie Zirngast presented in BALDY-RAMA a Baldyman presentation

A STEAMY THRILLER IN THE 'BASIC INSTINCT' MOULD

## PRET -A- PORTER U

Baldyman Pictures presents an Adrian Sington production a Jake Lingwood film starring B.Aldyman in Pret-A-Porter co-producer Humphrey Price costumes designed by Jean-Paul Gaultier music by Electric Light Orchestra edited by Clare Hulton production designer Christine Corton director of photography Chantal Noel based on the novel by Grianne Ashton screenplay by Julie Zirngast produced by Karen Ellison Vicky Johnson Katy Carrington Vicky Monk directed by Jake Lingwood presented in BALDY-RAMA a Baldyman presentation

A GLAMOROUS LOOK AT THE WORLD OF HIGH FASHION

## OUTBREAK PG

Baldyman Pictures presents an Adrian Sington production a Jake Lingwood film starring B.Aldyman in Outbreak co-producer Humphrey Price costumes designed by Jean-Paul Gaultier music by Electric Light Orchestra edited by Clare Hulton production designer Christine Corton director of photography Chantal Noel based on the novel by Grianne Ashton screenplay by Julie Zirngast produced by Karen Ellison Vicky Johnson Katy Carrington Vicky Monk directed by Jake Lingwood presented in BALDY-RAMA a Baldyman presentation

A HANDSOME SCIENTIST SEEKS A CURE FOR THE VIRUS THAT HAS SPOILED HIS LOOKS

**Yes, as you'll have gathered from the descriptions of the exciting, action packed films pictured on the previous page, I've bought a Camcorder! And after only 3 hours use I found I was able to write, direct and produce my own blockbuster movies every bit as well as Spielberg, Hitchcock or the studios of Metro-Goldwyn-Hair.**

There's no better way of creating an impression than by creeping up behind somebody with your camcorder and shouting 'Action' suddenly in their ear. Of course whilst the films I took of other people were superb there was always something missing on the screen. Then I suddenly realised what it was - yes **ME.** So as well as being the writer, director and producer I became the star as well.

### 1.CHOOSING A CAMCORDER
Picking the right Camcorder is vital. The simplest way is to find out which model your neighbour has and then buy the next more expensive one. Be sure to leave the empty box in an exposed place on top of your bin or outside your front gate so he'll see it when he comes home.

# HOW TO MAKE YOUR OWN SPECTACULAR FILM!

### 2.WRITING THE SCRIPT
Forget about the words, exotic locations are the key. Fortunately many are available locally.

### 3.MAKING THE FILM
What better way of indoctrinating you in the art of cinematography than by revealing my personal experiences as a film-maker. Over the page then is my diary of the first day's shooting of my latest epic, directed by and starring Yours Truly, Basil Aldyman in **'The Singing In The Bath Detective'**

*millionaires pad*

*chic penthouse*

*the rolling vistas of the serengetti*

IN THIS SCENE FROM 'OUTBREAK' ALL MANNER OF EXOTIC LOCATIONS CAN BE SEEN.

P.T.O.

# DIARY OF A MOVIE STAR!

**05.30**  First day of shooting on **'The Singing In The Bath Detective'**. The alarm goes and I drag myself out of bed. First chore of the day is to turn plain insignificant little me (ha!ha!) into the sex god you see on screen! So I place myself in the hands of some Hollywood style make-up experts.

**06.00**  Hair! And I'm stuck in a chair for 3 hours!

**09.00**  Eventually the salon opens so I pick my picnic stool up off the pavement and go in. I can tell I'm in for an all-embracing, comprehensive, thoroughgoing, meticulous, hair job!

**09.04**  Out at last!!

**09.15**  Into 'Wardrobe'! Four (rather pretty) girls fuss around me. I join in their jolly, sophisticated repartee as they try to find some flesh coloured underpants for me.

**09.30**  I leave 'What Everyone Wants'.

**09.31**  Discover my personal chauffer has disappeared. This is after me leaving specific instructions for him to wait for me <u>and</u> giving him a 5p tip for doing so! You just can't trust taxi drivers anymore! Fortunately all is not lost as I find **another** 5p in an envelope lying on the pavement marked 'For The Baldy Git' I'll keep the 5p for now but give it to that gentleman should I ever encounter him.

**10.00**  I arrive on 'location' - otherwise known as 'home'.

**10.05**  The next chore - dealing with the fan mail! There must be over 100 cards all from people urging me to 'break a leg!' I open them excitedly. Naturally there's one from 'Ken and Em' - the darlings! - nothing from Bob Hoskins but I expect he'll 'phone, and one from 'Dickie' ( a little bit smudged). No other post of note (except for a final demand from a greetings card firm).

**10.30**  Time to get started! As I'm directing myself in this film I go and inspect the 'set' or as it's described in the script 'the hero's bathroom'. I play a maverick detective who solves all his cases in the bath - actually modelled on 'Morse', who's a bit of a soak too. Doing most of my scenes in the bath was a conscious decision on my part. Those filmgoers who appreciate seeing the star brilliantly solve the crime can enjoy my skilled powers of deduction, while the female contingent get a chance to ogle my body.

**10.45**  Ready for the first 'take'. Although I have written to the police telling them I am making a film and requesting them to cordon off the street to reduce traffic noise, they have failed to carry out my instructions. I decide to take matters into my own hands.

**10.50**  Go outside. Use loud hailer to call for quiet. Several people come out to see what all the noise is about.

**10.55**  Back in bathroom! Shout 'Action' through loud hailer.

**10.55 - 11.10** Go completely deaf for 15 minutes.

**11.11** Turn volume down on loud hailer. Say 'Action' very quietly. Set camcorder to record. This is it!

**11.12** Put camcorder battery on charge. Wait.

**12.00** Battery still not charged. Decide to get ready for lunch. Professional caterers have been booked for 12.30. Go into make-up box and apply white hair & moustache, affect quavery old man's voice, get walking stick from 'props'.

**12.30** Open door to 'Meals on Wheels' lady. Accept tray of food.

**12.31** Remove old man's make-up and tuck into lunch.

**13.00** My batteries are recharged and so are the camcorders! It's time to get cracking.

**13.35** I'm in costume. I've learned my lines. The camcorder is set up on its tripod ready to capture the scene. I drop my bathrobe and climb into the bath!

**13.35** The 'phone rings. I leap out to answer it. It could be Madonna agreeing to do the walk-on part I offered her!

**13.50** Return to bathroom after long complex discussion about possible set for my next film. Texture, colour, lighting are all taken into consideration. 'Sophisticated Kitchens' say they'll send their rep round first thing in the morning.

**14.00** The big moment. I'm in the bath. As I turn to say my lines I discover that a large bar of soap on the bathside is partially obstructing the camera's view of me. Put soap on floor out of the way.

**14.01** Doorbell goes! It could be Pamela Anderson for her audition.

**14.05** Re-enter bathroom in bad mood after returning tray to 'Meals on Wheels' lady.

**14.05** Slip on soap.

**17.30** Regain consciousness.

**17.35** Fetch scissors and cut hole in shower-cap for large lump on head.

**17.40** Realise it's getting dark and there isn't enough light in the bathroom to shoot the scene! Throw open bathroom curtains. Then go outside, start up car, switch headlights onto full beam and point them through bathroom window.

**17.45** Back in bathroom. Drop robe for nude scene. Accidentally sit on scissors.

**17.45 - 17.50** Leap about rather a lot.

**18.00** Answer door to police investigating reports of a flasher.

**19.00** Spend night in cells.

# Mad dogs and Baldymen go out in the mid-day sun

| JULY | | | | | | |
|---|---|---|---|---|---|---|
| M | T | W | T | F | S | S |
| 1 | 2 | 3 | 4 | 5 | 6 | 7 |
| 8 | 9 | 10 | 11 | 12 | 13 | 14 |
| 15 | 16 | 17 | 18 | 19 | 20 | 21 |
| 22 | 23 | 24 | 25 | 26 | 27 | 28 |
| 29 | 30 | 31 | | | | |

| AUGUST | | | | | | |
|---|---|---|---|---|---|---|
| M | T | W | T | F | S | S |
| | | | 1 | 2 | 3 | 4 |
| 5 | 6 | 7 | 8 | 9 | 10 | 11 |
| 12 | 13 | 14 | 15 | 16 | 17 | 18 |
| 19 | 20 | 21 | 22 | 23 | 24 | 25 |
| 26 | 27 | 28 | 29 | 30 | 31 | |

# Fashionably Yours

## The Caviare of Catalogues

**Autumn–Winter**

# STYLES WHICH NEVER CHANGE

Fashion is a fickle mistress – but some styles just become classics. Here are just a couple of the perennial designs that transcend any trends.

**1 The Cardigan**
You'll never look out of place in this timeless creation from Kasual Kardies! Loose fit with handy pockets. Perfect for giving it a 'twirl'.
65% POLYESTER
35% MAN-MADE
**£9.99  L  XL  XXL**

**2 Duffle Coat**
Never mind the Sloane Ranger, meet the Sloane Rambo! The designer Duffle for the 'He-man' about town.
100% ITCHY WOOL
**BLACK ONLY**
**£10.99**

**3 Fashion Sandals**
No more sweaty feet on the dance floor with these!
Available in:
**BROWN LEATHER**
**PINK/CLEAR/BLUE**
**"JELLY"**
**£3.99 All sizes**

**GREAT VALUE**

**1 9.99**

**2 10.99 BLACK ONLY**

**3 3.99**

**"Breathe Easy"**

**SOCKS NOT INCLUDED**

# I PUT THE RUG IN RUGGED

**1** **14.⁹⁹**

PRICEY, BUT WORTH IT

**2** **9.⁹⁹**

**3** **12.⁹⁹**

**4** **2.⁹⁹**

BE WISE, ACCESSORISE!

**5** **2.⁹⁹**

If clothes were foreign languages denim would be spoken everywhere and I'd be fluent in all styles.

**1 Denim Jacket** Lightwight and casual. Zip up front. Includes two 'Armhole' features.
**£14.99**

**2 Denim Shirt** As above. Dry clean only. Iron well.
**£9.99**

**3 Denim Jeans** As above. Come with 'Everlasting' crease.
**£12.99**

**4 Denim Hat**
All sizes available. Don't forget to allow for thick hair when ordering.
**£2.99**

**5 Leather belt**
White only
**£2.99**

All Denim items 100% 'GGGRRRR!' and come in Ice Blue only.
Available in three sizes:
**MAN**
**XTRA-MAN**
**HUNK**

**6** **99ᴾ**

**7** **99ᴾ**

# SECOND HAND – FIRST CLASS!

Once you would be laughed at for buying clothes in a charity shop. Today, only admired for your thrift and good judgement. It's hard to believe but this second hand suit has hardly been worn. Made with 50% wool, 40% polyester and 10% mothballs, the designer labels say it all – 'Hep-worths', 'Jacksons', 'John Temple'.

**6 Jacket** available in **ORANGE, TURQUOISE, AQUA-MARINE** and **DUNG**.
**99p**

**7 Trousers** available in four colours **PLUM, TERRACOTTA, PAMPAS** and **TUNA**.
**99p**
This suit comes in one size only and fits all.

# SECOND HAND – FIRST CLASS!

Slinky Separates abound in the charity shop! These super-loose fashion slacks are a snip and come with a twill pattern, a pale stripe and a slight odour.

**1** Trousers 100% AIRTEX
Available in:
**CREAM YOGHURT HOUMOUS 49p**

Don't be afraid to Mix and Match! This 'Easy-on-the-Eye' top will make you look cool in summer… and super-cool at parties!

**2** Shirt
Available in an amazing two hundred colours. And that's just one shirt!

**1** 49p

**2** FREE

STAINS BECOME INVISIBLE ON THIS 'CAMOUFLAGE' FABRIC

PAY NOW, RECEIVE LATER!

# MAKING A SPLASH ON THE BEACH

Don't forget, the less you wear, the more it matters! On the beach you have to make a fashion statement with just one garment! So show off those legs in a glamourous pair of beach shorts. Don't forget they can be worn both smart and casual.

**1** **4.**99 SMART

**1** Beach shorts – smart
£4.99  XL  XXL  XXMCLXVII

**2** Beach shorts – casual
£39.99  XL  XXL  XXMCLXVII

**2** **39.**99 CASUAL

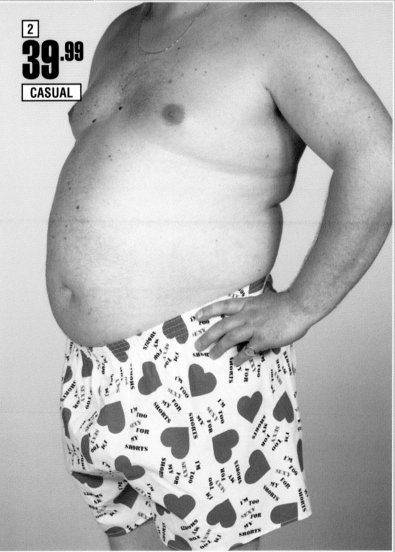

**3** **99p**
PANTS PROMO PRICE

PANTS PROMO PRICE

**4** **99p**

Once that tan has taken hold, slip into some sexy Mini-Briefs – the Y-fronts that put the 'Y' in 'Y Viva Espana!'

Pants come in all sizes:
**XXL   XL   L   M   S**
and an eye-watering **XS**

**3** Apple Mini-briefs
99p
**Second Hand price 49p**

**4** Paisley Mini Briefs
99p or 2 for £1

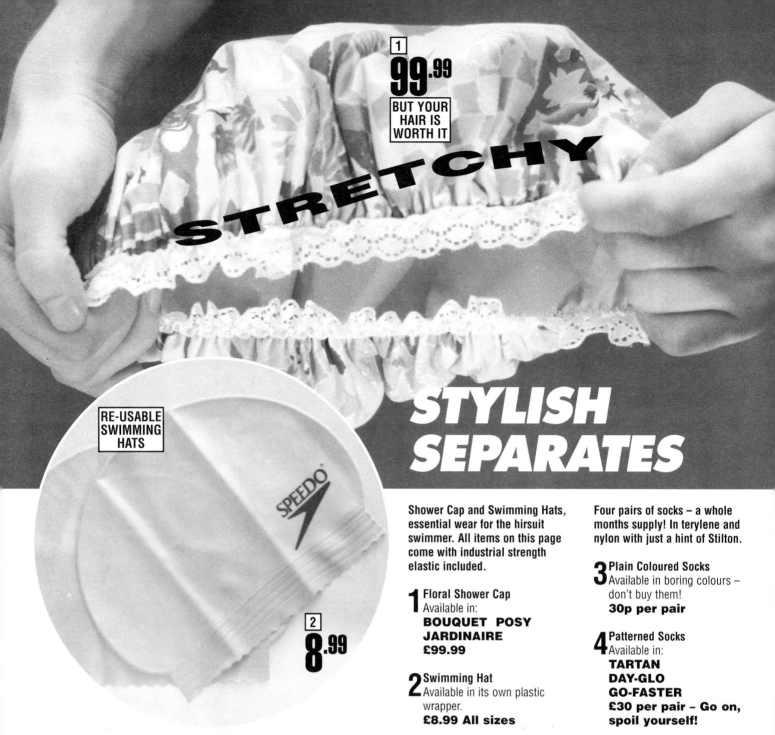

**1**

**99**.99

BUT YOUR HAIR IS WORTH IT

STRETCHY

RE-USABLE SWIMMING HATS

SPEEDO

**2**

**8**.99

# STYLISH SEPARATES

Shower Cap and Swimming Hats, essential wear for the hirsuit swimmer. All items on this page come with industrial strength elastic included.

**1** Floral Shower Cap
Available in:
**BOUQUET POSY JARDINAIRE**
**£99.99**

**2** Swimming Hat
Available in its own plastic wrapper.
**£8.99 All sizes**

Four pairs of socks – a whole months supply! In terylene and nylon with just a hint of Stilton.

**3** Plain Coloured Socks
Available in boring colours – don't buy them!
**30p per pair**

**4** Patterned Socks
Available in:
**TARTAN**
**DAY-GLO**
**GO-FASTER**
**£30 per pair – Go on, spoil yourself!**

**3**

**30**ᵖ
A PAIR

**4**

**30**.00
A PAIR

DO NOT IRON

DRY CLEAN ONLY

# THE ALDYMAN DIET PLAN

It's a well known fact that fat people don't make such a good impression as those who are lithe & slim. So you can imagine the panic that sets in in my house when, despite the fact I've been 'working out', all of a sudden I find I can't get into one of my favourite outfits!

The message is clear, time to Count the Calories! Yet even in this supposedly diet conscious age I am amazed by the number of basic food products still unavailable in reduced calorie form! It seems we can put a man on the moon (which incidentally is a very good way to achieve weight loss) but we still can't manufacture basic slimming foods! Just take a look at some of the products I was unable to purchase on my last calorie counting trip to the shops:

### THE LOW FAT EGG
### THE SUGAR FREE SUGAR LUMP
### THE SLIMLINE SWEET STOUT.

In the end I was forced to purchase a tin of 'LOW FAT ALPHABETTI SPAGHETTI', yet on opening it I discovered the letters F.A.T. no less than 17 times! Naturally I returned the tin to the shop.

## 1 Eating Out

Eating out is fraught with problems for the slimmer. Vegetarians can simply say 'I'm sorry, I don't eat meat' and instantly be provided with a choice of vegetarian dishes. What happens to the diner who says 'I'm sorry, I don't eat calories'! No equivalent 'nocalorie' menu exists! In this situation, however, it is still possible to give the **impression** of being on diet. If you see another diner about to tuck into chips, tut loudly, look superior and if necessary remove his plate! He will thank you for it later.

## 2 Lifestyle

Diet is often about lifestyle. If you enter a tall building and normally take the lift still do this! But whilst in the lift perform some strenuous jogging on the spot and arm stretching exercises. This will impress other lift users who will often get out and take the stairs!

## 3 Finally
### some simple tips to help you through!

**A** Don't weigh yourself everyday. Once a year is enough for me.

**B** If you've been good, give yourself a little treat. I find a visit to the hair salon a marvellous reward.

**C** Don't buy lots of biscuits and cakes if you've invited visitors round.

In my experience they often cancel at the last minute and you have to eat everything yourself! Tell your friends to bring their own food. This will show them what a slim, elegant, perfect example of manhood you are though it may be some time before you actually see them again.

# GARDEN

**My natural horticultural expertise means there's nothing 'square' about my Garden Corner! I was born with 'green fingers' ! Everything I touch seems to sprout luxurious growth. And what better way of making an impact in the neighbourhood than**

## SIMPLE TIPS

**1** Most horticultural experts favour late April/early May as the best time for pruning hedges and shrubs using an electric hedge-trimmer. Personally I favour six o'clock on a Sunday morning which, coincidentally, just happens to be the time when many of my neighbours seem to get up.

**2** Many gardening books recommend using straw as a mulch for strawberries. Take a tip from me. Save money by using hair clippings of which I have a natural abundance!

**3** Don't overstock your ornamental pond with plants and water lilies as these can end up completely covering the surface and preventing you from seeing your own reflection!

**4** If you have a brand spanking new mini-tractor, don't dirty it by filling it with garden rubbish and lawn clippings. Use it to go down to the post box or to nip across the street to borrow a pint of milk.

**5** Make sure you have a plentiful supply of garden twine. Then if any of your vegetables fail to impress you can pop down to the greengrocers, buy some larger examples and tie them onto your own plants. No one will notice the difference - but do make sure the neighbours see you picking them and walking proudly into the kitchen!

**6** Finally don't bother listening to 'Gardeners' Question Time, on the radio. They insist they employ experts but they haven't invited me on once!

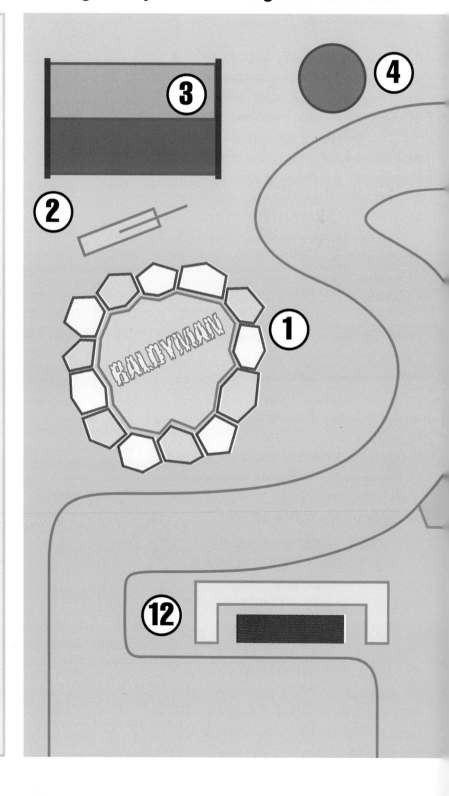

# CORNER

**by turning your garden into a mass of colour! Red, yellow, purple, mauve, pink, orange & violet - my gardening trousers are the talk of the street! And now you too can be the envy of gardeners everywhere if you follow my six simple tips!**

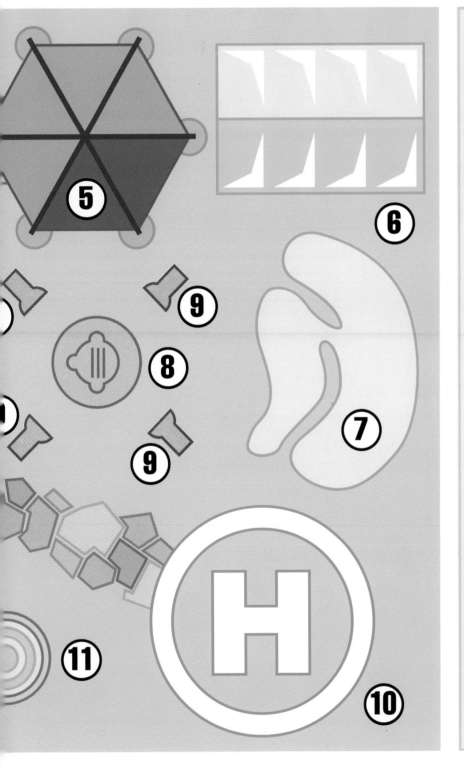

## KEY TO GARDEN

1. Unpretentious rockery with delightful flower arrangement.

2. Weather vane with little lumberjack chopping wood - surprisingly the only one in our street showing what a style leader I am!

3. Garden Shed. Nothing fancy. Creosoted wood finish with stone cladding, coach lamps and rustic nameplate saying 'Dunweedin'.

4. Compost Heap. Environmentally sound way of recycling hair clippings etc.

5. The Hanging Gardens of Aldyman.

6. Greenhouse containing many rare and exotic plants such as lettuces, tomatoes and rhubarb.

7. Exquisite artificial lake created when I was metal detecting over the water main.

8. Marble bust of myself.

9. Floodlights directed at marble bust (automatically turn on at night).

10. Heli-pad for possible Royal Visit!

11. Bird bath with a difference! (How many do you know with their own wave machine!)

12. Barbecue. Built with honey sandstone brick and pebble-dashed to withstand hot fat splashes from exploding sausages.

# ON THE ROAD

**The car you drive says something about you and in motoring I've always put style first. From my very first Austin Allegro throught to my twin-cam Citroen 2CV, I've always gone for class.**

With so many modern cars looking the same, however, it's easy to become anonymous on the roads – and anonymous is certainly not a description I'd settle for! There's nothing more satisfying than seeing heads turn as you drive past – something I became regularly accustomed to when I had my two-tone lime green and orange Lada estate.

So how can today's motorist of distinction create a stir on the bland highways of the 1990s? The answer is to…

## BUY A CLASSIC CAR!

There are many Classic Cars on the market and that dream car you've always hankered after may be available more cheaply than you think, whether it's an E-Type or a Silver Cloud, both of which I have owned at one time (SEE PICTURES).

There are many advantages to owning a Classic Car. Firstly it entitles you to join a Classic Car Club. These clubs supply essential equipment for the Classic Car owner like myself. On buying your Classic Car you'll find you require the following:-

| | |
|---|---|
| **BADGED BASEBALL CAP** | **BADGED FILOFAX** |
| **BADGED SPORTS UMBRELLA** | **BADGED SWEATSHIRT** |
| **BADGED FOUNTAIN PEN** | **BADGED KEY FOB** |

All of which I purchased when I joined the ASTON MARTIN OWNERS CLUB. Many an attractive young lady was only too delighted to accept the offer of a lift home from a man with an Aston Martin key fob! Imagine her surprise on discovering it was actually a Morris Minor I owned! (Strangely, the Morris Minor key fob never had the same effect.)

A final word of warning. Classic Cars do break so it's helpful if, like me, you're an expert mechanic. You have to know exactly what is wrong with your car and how to fix it – so that when you summon the AA you are able to give the rescue man the full benefit of your advice while he's working.

The 'E' Type Bubble car

The Sinclair C5 'Silver cloud'

# CUSTOMISING YOUR CAR

**Is your everyday car indistinguishable from every other? If you want to get noticed on the highway the answer is to customise it! Here are a few suggestions from yours truly!**

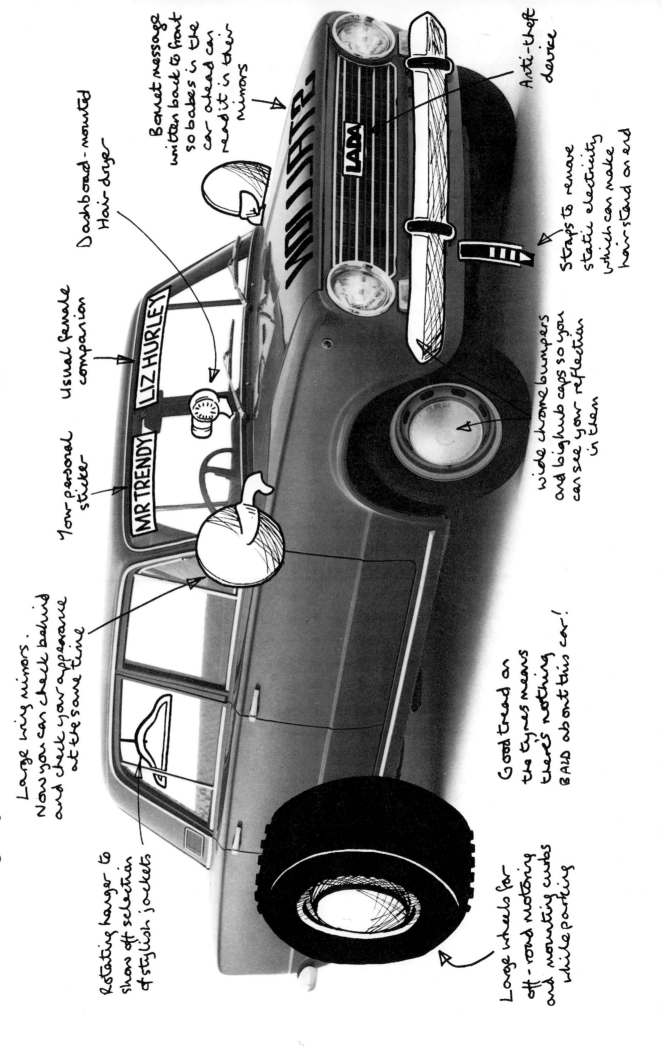

Bonnet message written back to front so babes in the car ahead can read it in their mirrors

Anti-theft device

Straps to remove static electricity which can make hair stand on end

Wide chrome bumpers and big hub caps so you can see your reflection in them

Dashboard-mounted Hair dryer

Usual female companion

Your personal sticker

Large wing mirrors. Now you can check behind and check your appearance at the same time

Rotating hanger to show off selection of stylish jackets

Good tread on the tyres means there's nothing BALD about this car!

Large wheels for off-road motoring and mounting curbs while parking

# GET STUCK INTO STICKERS

A good driver will always show consideration for the car behind. Whether you're held up at the lights, stuck in a traffic jam ... or simply hogging the middle of the road, make sure your back window contains some stylish reading material. Here are the stickers currently sported by my rear screen!

My other car is being driven by **Naomi Campbell**

**CAR PARK PASS**
STUD-U-LIKE
Fitness Centre

I'M A RADIO **1** FAN

## THE LIONS OF LONGLEAT HAVE SEEN ME

LOOK OUT FOR HAIR SIGNALS

I'VE BOOGIED AT CLUB TROPICANA SKEGNESS

If you're going bald the best thing to do is to simply admit it! There's nothing more pathetic than a man absurdly trying to hide his condition behind a ridiculous sweep of hair! To put it bluntly - a balding fool and the hair just above his ear are soon parted!

If you're bald - admit it! Come out of the wardrobe! Accept what you are and who you are! You'll feel 100% better for it! Believe me, I know! I once had a friend in this position.

Fortunately I still have a full head of hair but I know how tragic life can be for baldies who refuse to accept and even try to hide their condition. I want to help them, and that's why I'm devoting this page of the book to...

# OUTING FAMOUS BALDIES

Valerie Singleton — All those years with the Blue Peter guinea pig on her head

70's Glam Rock icons ABBA — in reality ABBALD!

Mark Thatcher exposed as Mark NoThatcher

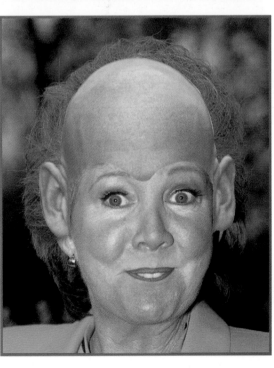

Someone's in for a surprise on their Blind Date!

# GETTING AWAY FROM IT ALL

I've found that there's no better way to impress my neighbours than by going on holiday. They're always impatient for me to be off - probably excited by the prospect of receiving a picture postcard of some exotic hotspot from Yours Truly! If you want to earn a reputation as a jet-setting globetrotter like me, simply take a couple of foreign holidays a year. You'll soon be regarded as a complete cosmopolitan - even though you've never actually visited Cosmopolia !

## WINTER BREAKS

Where better to go for a winter holiday than Klosters - the playground of the rich and famous! Even here, however, it pays to know where the 'in' places are! Fortunately, now you can take the guesswork out of your booking by using my painstakingly researched guide.

# GUIDE TO THE LODGES
Choose your ski lodge with this easy to follow handy guide. Each hotel is rated according to ambience and facilities, and awarded points in the form of

The more the better!

### THE ALPINE HORN
A modern multi-storey hotel but what attracted me to it was the tasteful traditional log cabin cladding on the front. All rooms are equipped with 3 speed hair driers and trouser presses for getting the ultimate creases into those ski pants. All mod cons means -

### THE KUCKOO KABIN
I instantly felt at home here. Everyone gets their own chalet - never mind Hi-de-Hi, it's more like Hi-de-Ski! Instead of Yellowcoats, however, it's men in white coats who seem to take you around everywhere. A little restrictive -

### THE SAUNA & SNOWSTORM
Princess Di once stayed here so it's an obvious must for -

### THE FROSTBITTEN TOE
Fergie stayed here. NO POINTS.

## Checking In to your Ski Lodge
When you arrive at your chosen hotel make sure you are wearing a thick, woolly balaclava, scarf and goggles. This allows you to write RICHARD GERE in the hotel register and assures you of excellent room service. There are usually one or two people with broken limbs lying about in the hotel lobby so have a biro handy to sign RICHARD GERE on their plaster too. If you're not sure what Richard Gere's signature looks like, here are a few of my efforts:-

## First Day On The Slopes
Klosters can be busy at the height of the season so in order to get the attention you deserve it pays to wear the best designer ski wear. I favour suits bearing the words "PALACE"; "BY APPOINTMENT"; or simply "E.R.". (Words to be avoided on a ski suit are "EDDIE" and "EAGLE".)

You need to look cool on the slopes and even in winter the sun can be surprisingly strong, so take precautions. If you don't want a burnt forehead wear a headband; sunburn on the nose can be prevented by applying some Factor 25 gel; and to avoid red raw, sore, peeling cheeks don't come down the ski slope on your bum.

At the start of the run all eyes will be on you so don't be afraid to show off. For instance if you find yourself standing next to a hulking six foot downhill racer with all the proper equipment the crowd will be impressed if you give him some advice before he sets off. Tell him to lean forward, arms slightly out and brace himself - then there's very little likelihood of the ski lift taking him by surprise.

## Ski Instructors
Many hotels will supply you with your own ski instructor. - usually called Claude or Hans. Dismiss them at once. Girls won't be impressed if they see you clinging to the hand of an instructor all the time. (If your ski instructor happens to be called Monique, ignore this advice and spend as much time with her as you can!)

Remember you're there to create an impression, so on your first day go straight to the top of the most challenging run, push yourself off and enjoy it!

## Medical Insurance
You may need this. Be sure you have completed a form before you set off ... and don't sign it Richard Gere.

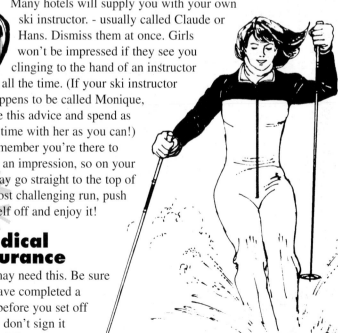

# You too can be...
## The KING of KARAOKE

Many people believe that Karaoke is a pastime indulged in by self-obsessed, talentless show offs. However, I like it! It gives me a chance to 'let my hairs down' and, most of all, to make the opposite sex swoon as I croon! I became 'King of Karaoke' through a mixture of natural talent, stunning good looks and, of course, hard work! But I am willing to pass on a few tips so that YOU will not make a fool of yourself.

### TIP NUMBER ONE
### Always dress for the occasion!

All the great singers of our time chose stage outfits which gave them instant recognition, meaning they could never be confused with another singer – for instance 'Old Blue Eyes' himself, Elvis Presley.

### TIP NUMBER TWO
### You must wear clothes that show off your best features.

Choosing my best features was difficult as they're all pretty wonderful but I eventually decided on…

Having identified these it was time to pick an outfit that would flatter them. I recommend skin tight trousers and an open shirt. Be very aware of the visible panty line and avoid this by not pulling your pants too far up over your stomach … and ensuring that your shirt is *not* tucked into the pants!

### TIP NUMBER THREE
### Learn to move well on stage.

Pelvic thrusts should be used extensively (especially during songs like 'Welcome Home' and 'I'd Like To Teach The World To Sing'.) If you're not confident about pelvic thrusts, spend a little time practising them in front of a mirror – say ten or twelve hours a day.

### TIP NUMBER FOUR
### Don't over-rehearse.

I personally have found that, very occasionally, if you are too good at Karaoke, the compere will not allow you on stage. Or he may even try and push you off after only ten or twelve songs! If this should happen keep your dignity, relinquish the microphone and leave the stage. When you do this I guarantee the cheers of the audience ringing in your ears will be all you need to confirm your belief that you are indeed a great Karaoke talent!

**My Karaoke Top Five**

1. Hair   2. Eleanor Wigby   3. Dreadlock Holiday
4. Save All Your Tresses For Me
5. These Roots Were Made For Walking

# CATEGORICALLY YOURS!

If, like me, you are an individual, a 'one-off', quite simply an exceptional example of humanity, you will probably not fit into any of the current 'people categories'.

So if you're not a :–

**DINKY**
Double Income
No Kids Yet

a **YUPPIE**
Young Upwardly-mobile
Professional

or an **OPTIE**
Over-mortgaged Post Thatcherite
Individual

yet would still like to create an impression by belonging to a group, why not join me . . .

**H**andsome

**A**ccomplished

**I**ntelligent

**R**espected

**I**ndividual

. . . and become a

# HAIRI !

# BODY LANGUAGE
## No.2 - THE JOB INTERVIEW

How The Right
Body Language
Can Help You
Get That Job

**Job Interviews are all
about first impressions! Naturally, I
don't have any problems on that score as
most people are completely bowled over by
me the first time we
meet. But if you're in
the least bit awkward,
shy, or lacking in self
confidence - or perhaps even downright
dull, boring and
tedious - then using
the right body language could alter your
career prospects
overnight.**

## ON ENTERING
## THE ROOM

**❶** Let your confident body
language send out signals
that, in you, they've got
the right man for the job.

**2** Don't sit down without being asked.

Especially if there isn't a chair.

Using the right body language you can convey total honesty and openness.

**3** Open palms – **RIGHT**

**4** Open flies – **WRONG**

# WHAT TO DO WITH YOUR HANDS

**5** A lot of people are unsure of where to put their hands during a job interview.

**6** The answer is to fold them neatly in your lap. This also solves the problem created in **4**.

## STRESS YOUR GOOD POINTS

**7** Draw attention to what you consider your finest attributes.

# POSTURE AND DRESS

**8** Showing too much leg isn't just a problem for women. It could lose the job for a man too!

**9** Unless the job happens to be with the Metropolitan Police.

**Are You Dancing?**

*Strictly Baldroom* ⑮

# My World of Wine

In order to be recognised as a true sophisticate like myself it's necessary to demonstrate one's mastery of the world of wine. What better way to impress in company than by displaying your grasp of the grape? Follow my simple guide and you can feel confident of picking the right plonk at any social occasion!

## IN THE RESTAURANT

A meal with friends in a restaurant is the perfect place to show off your superior knowledge. Forget the fact you are simply a guest and not the leader of the party and take charge right away. Demand to see the wine list! Spend time reading it, making appropriate noises of pleasure, surprise, and disapproval. Ignore any noises of impatience coming from the rest of your party - when they taste your choice of wine they'll be showering you with compliments and gratitude!!

Once you've selected the perfect bottle always make sure that you are the one who gets to taste the wine. If there's six of you in the party this means that at least you'll get a little bit more than the others.

A point to bear in mind here is that certain types of wine go better with certain dishes. The clue is often to be found in the name of the food, as demonstrated by the table below.

| FOOD | CORRECT WINE |
| --- | --- |
| Lamb | Lambrusco |
| Burgers | Burgundy |
| Spaghetti | Wormser Leibfraumorgen |
| Breast of Chicken | Bristol Cream |

As the evening progresses someone else at the table may wish to order a bottle too. Let him do this, but be prepared to criticise his choice when it arrives! Here your knowledge of vintages can come into play! Some wines are for drinking young, others are for laying down and keeping. If he has ordered a wine you consider should be kept, refuse to let him open it and insist on taking it home to put in your cellar for safety. This might cause some irritation at the table but remember **you** are the expert. Be firm. Even if it means you are asked to leave and end up drinking the bottle on your own at home later, be reassured by the knowledge that those extra couple of hours will have allowed the wine to mature correctly.

## THE DINNER PARTY GUEST

Imagine you are a guest at someone else's dinner party. The host (or more likely hostess!) pours you out a glass of wine. You have told the other guests that you are a connoisseur so don't simply accept it with no comment! They will not be expecting that! Take a large mouthful, swill it round your gums noisily and then spit it out onto the carpet. They won't be expecting that either but you will have made an impression.

Next you should describe the wine in detail but don't simply use the standard expressions, such as saying it has 'a good nose' - say it has nice ears and a charming smile as well.

Occasionally another - usually male! - member of the company will try to challenge your mastery of the subject by saying that a Leibfrau-milch is a white wine from Germany and not, as you have correctly stated, a sweet red from Ireland. This is where a knowledge of wine simply becomes wine snobbery! Ignore him and turn your back. There is only one place for your 'nose' for the rest of the evening, and that is in the air!

## TASTINGS AND WINE CLUBS

Having been a regular attender of the Saturday morning wine tastings offered by my local off licence, I was disappointed when these were suddenly terminated and I began to find the door to the off licence mysteriously locked whenever I appeared. More recently a local wine club advertised a 'Night for Wine Buffs'. Naturally I went along well-prepared only to be told to leave the premises, take my bottle of £1.99 Hock with me and put some clothes on! A true connoisseur will ignore these setbacks!

## BUYING GUIDE

If you still don't feel confident enough to practise your skills in public, here is my expert guide to the most famous wine growing regions of the world. A glance through this and you'll know all there is to know about choosing and drinking wine!

## THE WINE GROWING REGIONS

### FRANCE
Ooh La La! The wines of France! Or as we experts call them 'French' wines. Women love French wines, especially champagne which they think is 'tres romantique!'. If you can't afford champagne then just order any bottle of French wine and treat it as though it **is** champagne. You'll be surprised at the reactions you get in restaurants when you grab your £2.49 bottle of Cotes du Rhone, leap up onto the table, give it a right good shaking and point it at the head waiter.Don't be sur-prised if you're asked to leave at this point - it'll simply be proof that the restaurant doesn't know how to treat its wines!

### ITALY
There are three basic Italian wines - Valpollicella, Mafioso and Pavarotti. My particular favourite is 'Mafioso' as, when I whisper this to wine waiters in Italian restaurants, I invariably get excellent service and often receive no bill!

### GERMAN
German wines are a bit of a minefield. They all have names like 'Bad-bergzabener Bernkastler Kurfursterley Grosskarlbarcher Spatlese Schloss Saarfelser' and if you are afflicted by a particularly severe attack of hay fever while sitting in the restaurant you could find your-self ordering an extremely expensive bottle by accident! Another prob-lem is that half of them sound like football teams - there's not a great deal of difference between 'Deinheimer Paterhof' and 'Borussia Munchengladbach'- so you could find yourself doing the German equivalent of ordering a half karafe of Nottingham Forest or, worse still, a magnum of Crewe Alexandra. Take my advice as a connoisseur and leave the Tetonic Tipple to others!

### THE NEW WORLD
The true connoisseur will steer well clear of these! How could the words 'Australia' and 'class' ever be linked together?

# Penny for the best-dressed guy

**SEPTEMBER**

| M | T | W | T | F | S | S |
|---|---|---|---|---|---|---|
| 30 | | | | | | |
| 2 | 3 | 4 | 5 | 6 | 7 | 1 |
| 9 | 10 | 11 | 12 | 13 | 14 | 8 |
| 16 | 17 | 18 | 19 | 20 | 21 | 15 |
| 23 | 24 | 25 | 26 | 27 | 28 | 22 |
| | | | | | | 29 |

**OCTOBER**

| M | T | W | T | F | S | S |
|---|---|---|---|---|---|---|
| | 1 | 2 | 3 | 4 | 5 | 6 |
| 7 | 8 | 9 | 10 | 11 | 12 | 13 |
| 14 | 15 | 16 | 17 | 18 | 19 | 20 |
| 21 | 22 | 23 | 24 | 25 | 26 | 27 |
| 28 | 29 | 30 | 31 | | | |

**NOVEMBER**

| M | T | W | T | F | S | S |
|---|---|---|---|---|---|---|
| | | | | 1 | 2 | 3 |
| 4 | 5 | 6 | 7 | 8 | 9 | 10 |
| 11 | 12 | 13 | 14 | 15 | 16 | 17 |
| 18 | 19 | 20 | 21 | 22 | 23 | 24 |
| 25 | 26 | 27 | 28 | 29 | 30 | |

**Swell Gel** Probably The Best Laquer in the World

# RELATIVE VALUES

**MRS ALDYMAN, MOTHER** You never forget, no matter how old you get. The smoothness of his pink, baldy head, that warm, slightly cheesey smell and the pudgy, puse wrinkly face. No you never forget. Well, I'm hardly likely to, am I? It was only yesterday after all. That's when "B", as I always call him - because he can be a real "B" of a son - popped his head round the door while I was doing his weekly wash and told me I had to write 200 words about our relationship. "Two hundred!" I said, "I could do it in two but they would't be able to print it!" I confess I wasn't in the best of tempers because the little darling had left me a note insisting I give his shirt collars a good scrub by hand! How on earth he managed to get Brylcreem on them is beyond me!

What do I remember about him as a child? He was always a bit of a loner. He was certainly never close to his father. Mainly because his father emigrated to Ecuador minutes after he was born. This meant in the early years we had a particularly close relationship. I still remember laying out his clean white vests and powdering his little bottom - mainly because the other boys in the school changing room used to be looking over my shoulder and laughing.

"B" was a conscientious pupil and was always proudly bringing me home things from school - athletes foot, verrucas, but strangely enough, never nits! I remember the day he arrived home bent double on his hands and knees having crawled all the way! I was afraid he'd suffered a terrible injury on the sports field but it turned out to be less serious. The poor dear was learning to tie his shoelaces and had accidentally threaded his hair throught the laceholes!

Like many children he had lots of imaginary friends! Barefoot Tommy, wee Mary Lou, Big Bill. Unlike most kids' imaginary friends, however, they were real children - it's just that "B" imagined they were his friends.

It's a mother's instinct to nurture and as he grew older I could tell that my son's personality was crying out for love and attention, so I bought him a budgie. The budgie's arrival made "B" so happy. He would spend hour after hour by its cage, gazing lovingly at his own reflection in Joey's little mirror. Eventually, Joey, fed up with never getting a chance to preen himself, escaped. Poor "B" was inconsolable. Joey had smashed the mirror first.

The teenage years saw the start of temper tantrums and bumfluff. With "B" the tantrums and the bumfluff were usually connected. Most normal children start to grow bodyhair during puberty and "B" was no exception, except that he tried to grow it long enough to comb over his head. I seem to remember he was the only boy in the school who had his armpits in ponytails. He always seemed to be obsessed with hair and I remember the day I came home and found him standing in front of the mirror trying on one of my wigs! I gave him a good telling off - and made him take off my dress and high heels too!

Looking back there have been many memorable days in our relationship. The day he graduated from college, the day he started his first job, the day he won the award for top sales trainee of the year. But for me the happiest day of all was the day he finally left home. I remember saying to him, "Just think - Freedom! Independence! For this first time the chance to stamp your own personality in your own space! At last I'll have all these things - now GET OUT!!"

Of course, the bond between a mother and her son is a lasting link. A mother still likes to be needed and a son can never forget all the things his mother did for him - like washing, ironing, mending and writing notes excusing him from meetings with his bank manager because he has a cold! All these things keep the two of us in touch and lead me to the conclusion many mothers must have arrived at, especially me - "A son like "B" is a nuisance!"

**BASIL ALDYMAN, SON** I don't believe it! Have you seen what the old witch has written about me! From now on she can whistle for my washing - at least once she's got those Brylcreem stains of my collars. ∎

# INNOVATIONS

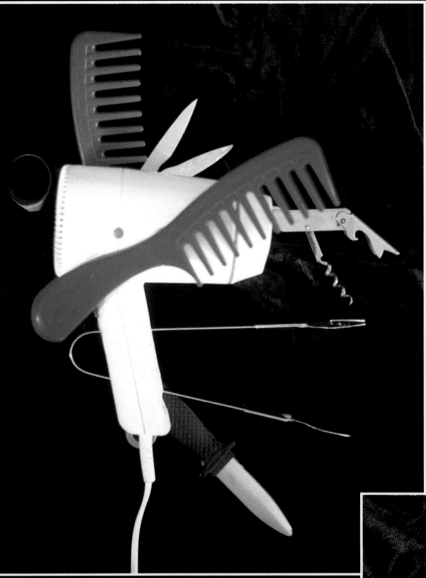

In the modern fast-moving world of today it's vital to keep abreast of new technology. I pride myself on being on top of all the latest scientific developments - from widescreen c.d. to hyperactive video - and in my own modest workshop I confess to having designed & built some remarkable gadgetry of my own.

Strangely enough, when I have approached the top technical journal of the Scientific World – 'Innovations' magazine – little interest has been shown in my inventions.

Their loss is your gain as I now bring you some of my most successful creations.

### SWISS ARMY HAIRDRYER

Those of you, like myself, whose reputation depends on their appearance will recognise the dilemma. While abroad, a small gust of wind has slightly shifted the impeccable coiffeur it took hours to create. That's where my handy **SWISS ARMY HAIRDRYER** comes into play. It contains curling tongs, nasal hair trimmer, comb, hair gel, shower cap plus electric toothbrush and manicure set as well as the thing for taking stones out of horses' hooves.

### COLOUR CO-ORDINATOR

A fantastic fashion accessory that helps you infallibly decide how to match socks, trousers, shirt and sweater.

## EVERLASTING RUBBER STAMP

The name of Aldyman has always been important in the world's past i.e. from the day I was born. This is why it is with great pleasure I introduce my **EVERLASTING RUBBER STAMP**. Visiting neighbours or clients need no longer worry over my name, now that it can be found on all my napkins, cushions, and each individual sheet of toilet paper.

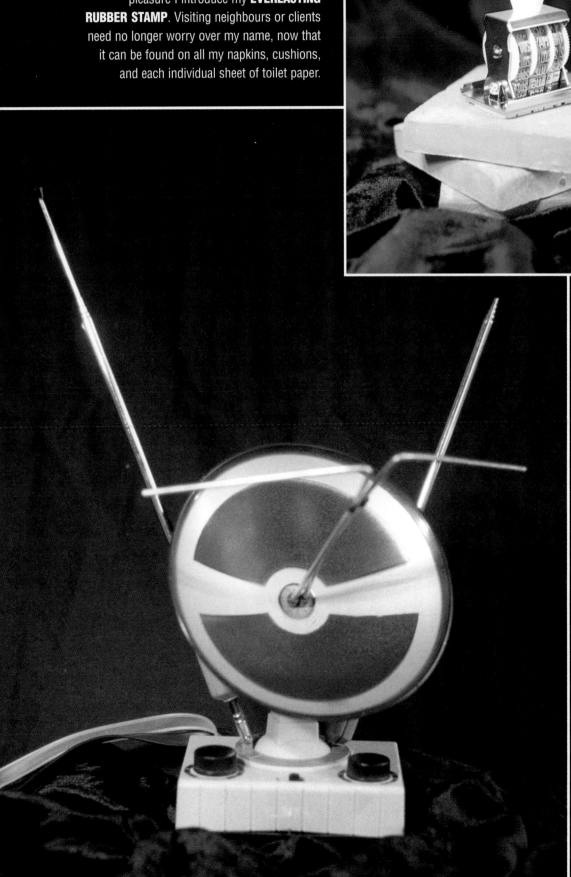

## REMOTE-CONTROLLED SHOPPING TROLLEY

Shopping at 'What Every Man Wants' or any other top fashion store can be a bit of a drag if you have to carry all the stuff home. That's why I've invented the **REMOTE-CONTROLLED SHOPPING TROLLEY TRANSMITTER.**
Attach it with sucker devices to any common or garden shopping trolley and it will follow you all over the department, and transport thirty polyester polo-necks. A successful test over that last month proved that only those in a 500 yard radius with a heart pacemaker were in any danger.

# **A**CQUIRE **S**UPERIOR **S**KILLS

**PLAY A MUSICAL INSTRUMENT**

**It's hard to imagine someone more popular at parties than me. What's my secret? Being able to play a musical instrument!**

Picture the scene. The party is in full swing. People are drinking, chatting and dancing to music. Then I come in, switch off the CD and start to play the piano! Imagine everyone's joy and delight as I go through my favourite pieces!

**RUG TIME**

**HAIR ON A G-STRING**

**BOOGIE WIGGIE**

You'll never find **me** in the kitchen at parties. I still find it puzzling why everyone else ends up there.

# CHOOSING YOUR INSTRUMENT

There are musical instruments to suit everyone's taste, from the violin to the comb and paper. Every instrument has an individual 'feel' however, so many famous musicians build up large collections.

Choosing the right instrument for you can be a minefield. I like the piano because of its deep and resonant sound, the variety of pieces specially written for it, but mostly because I can see myself in the highly polished lid while I'm playing.

Nigel Kennedy's collection of violins

My collection of COMBS!

## STARTING TO PLAY!

Let's assume you're a complete novice! Don't worry, so was I at one time, yet now I'm up there with the finest keyboard players in the country… and Linda McCartney. In fact I've long believed that many famous keyboard players secretly watch my technique and copy my style – especially the infectious smile I display whilst playing.

The good news is it's easy to become a good piano player. The secret is to START YOUNG! Both Mozart and I started when we were only four years old, so if you're already older than that give up and try another instrument.

The Original !

Where did this cheeky chappie get his smile?

## THE GUITAR

Demonstrating one's prowess on the guitar is a great way to impress the ladies – believe me, I know! All you need to do is wear a chunky sweater, buy a 'Peter, Paul and Mary Songbook' and hang about the guitar section in music shops, nodding sagely at the assistants and shaking your head at the people trying out the instruments. (Always have a bandaged hand in case somebody asks you to play a piece you consider beneath you!)

## OTHER INSTRUMENTS

There are far too many instruments for me to be able to cover all of them in the pages of this book. I, of course, am a master of them all and find that a good way of demonstrating this is to put a cassette of orchestral music in my walkman and practice conducting. Good places to do this are on crowded trains or buses, on park benches, or, in fact, at live concerts of classical music! It's amazing to see how many members of the orchestra watch **my** arms rather than those of the conductor – even though I'm listening to a totally different piece of music! Often a recital has to be halted while I am asked to move out of the eyeline of the musicians. Usually this instruction is taken too far and I am deposited on the street! I am left with the consoling thought that at least the audience has had the opportunity to see a **real** maestro at work!

# Happy kissmas – the start of a very long wait

| | | | DECEMBER | | | |
|---|---|---|---|---|---|---|
| **M** | **T** | **W** | **T** | **F** | **S** | **S** |
| 30 | 31 | | | | | **1** |
| 2 | 3 | 4 | 5 | 6 | **7** | **8** |
| 9 | 10 | 11 | 12 | 13 | **14** | **15** |
| 16 | 17 | 18 | 19 | 20 | **21** | **22** |
| 23 | 24 | 25 | 26 | 27 | **28** | **29** |